The Book of
Litcham *with* Lexham
& Mileham

A Celebration of Three Breckland Villages

Litcham Historical & Amenity Society

HALSGROVE

First published in Great Britain in 2002

British Library Cataloguing-in-Publication Data
A CIP record for this title is available from the British Library

ISBN 1 84114 190 9

HALSGROVE

Halsgrove House
Lower Moor Way
Tiverton, Devon EX16 6SS
Tel: 01884 243242
Fax: 01884 243325
email: sales@halsgrove.com
website: http://www.halsgrove.com

Frontispiece photograph: *Mr Pigg, Mileham Post Office and general stores, c.1910. The pony and trap was used
by Miss Pigg to deliver goods in the village.*

Printed and bound in Great Britain by Bookcraft Ltd, Midsomer Norton.

FOREWORD

It gives me great pleasure to commend to you *The Book of Litcham with Lexham and Mileham*. So much of our history gets lost in time and goes unrecorded, but in this case we are fortunate that the Litcham Historical & Amenity Society has taken the initiative in writing this history of three small villages in the Upper Nar Valley; known locally as 'Norfolk's Holy Land' due to the large number of abbeys, priories and churches founded in Saxon and Norman times. We are, indeed, lucky that we live in such a beautiful and historic part of Norfolk.

I am sure that this is a book which will give great pleasure to present and future generations and will be a valuable contribution to the recording of the history of Norfolk.

N.W.D. Foster, Lord of the Manor, 2002.

Litcham village sign with the almshouses to the rear, which were demolished in the 1950s.

Front Street, Litcham, 1920.

CONTENTS

Photograph showing the cattle that once grazed in Lexham Park.

An aerial photograph of the village of Litcham, 1988.

ACKNOWLEDGEMENTS

This book was compiled by members of the Litcham Historical & Amenity Society. The society was formed as a result of changes occurring in the village due to the demolition of old buildings and the construction of new properties. Founded in 1990, the principal aim of the society is to collect and collate artefacts, photographs and records in order to better preserve the history of the village. All of the members are volunteers who have a keen interest in local history.

In 1991 the society opened the Litcham Museum which houses collections from Litcham, Lexham and Mileham. This includes over 1,000 photographs covering the period from 1860 to the time of writing in 2002.

The villages of Litcham and Mileham are designated conservation areas which enables the society to work closely with the Parish Council in viewing all planning applications.

The Litcham Historical & Amenity Society is deeply indebted to Mr Stephen Olley of the Mid Norfolk Picture Archive, Mr T. Burchell, Mr R. Butler-Stoney and Shirley Proyer for their hard work and dedication.

The society would also like to thank all of those people who have helped with the compilation of this book including Mr and Mrs Green, Mr Norman Wagg, John Bell and Mr and Mrs Andrews. All information contained within the book is correct to the best of our knowledge and we apologise if any errors have been made.

It has been a great pleasure to produce this book on the villages of Litcham, Lexham and Mileham.

Ron Shaw, Chairman, 2002.

Lexham Hall is a Grade II listed building. Parts of the Hall date from 1650, it was added to in 1680 and 1780 and was restored in 1946/47.

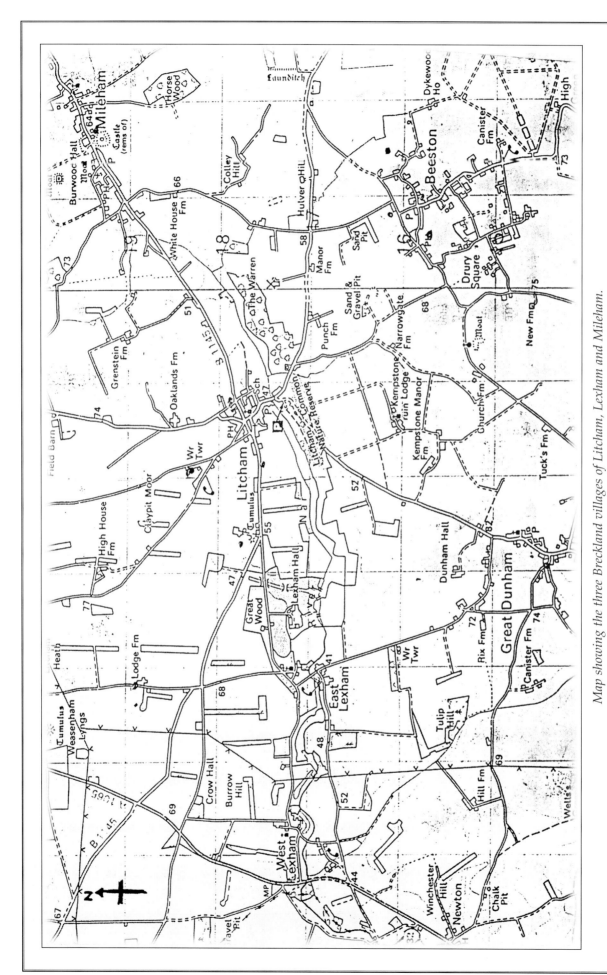

Map showing the three Breckland villages of Litcham, Lexham and Mileham.

ONE

THREE BRECKLAND VILLAGES

The village of Litcham is described in the Domesday Book as 'a market town in the centre of Norfolk'. It is a conservation village situated on the B1145 highway between Kings Lynn and Norwich. This was once the King's Lynn/Norwich/Great Yarmouth stagecoach route and horses were changed at The Bull Inn, parts of which still exist.

There is a wealth of listed buildings in the village, each with its own interesting history, including the twelfth-century church and priory. Just outside the village Roman settlements and roads are evident and an extensive collection of coins and artefacts from the surrounding area is housed in the local museum.

East Lexham is situated half a mile west of Litcham and is the seat of the lord of the manor of

Litcham. It has a fine hall, rebuilt in 1946/47 by the late Mr W.R.B. Foster and more recently by Mr N.W.D. Foster. The estate has excellent woodlands and buildings and a fine example of a Saxon round-tower church. Another round-tower church can be found down the road at West Lexham.

Mileham is situated a mile or so from Litcham in the opposite direction from Lexham and is a conservation village. At the east end of the village there stands a very fine church and there are also remnants of a castle. Amenities include a Post Office, a general store, a horticultural nursery run by the Cason family and an excellent primary school. The population of the ancient village of Mileham is little changed from the 546 recorded in *White's Directory* of 1864.

The Street, Mileham, looking east.

Above: Aerial view of Mileham. The Oak public house is on the right; it is no longer licensed.

Below: View to the south from Litcham Church Tower, 1935.

VIEWS FROM LITCHAM
CHURCH TOWER, 1978.

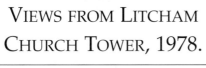

Above: *Chestnut Corner, Litcham, 1905. The two figures in the picture are Mr and Mrs Burton.*

Below: *Front Street, Litcham, c.1955.*

*Bull Hill, showing Mr Symonds (cobbler),
The Bull Inn and the cycle shop.*

HISTORICAL LITCHAM

The recorded history of Litcham is scant and explains little of its origins or subsequent growth. A settlement was originally established on higher ground above the marshy valley bottom, near a point where the River Nar could be forded. It soon developed as a central route to the extent that during the reign of Edward I Litcham received the right to hold a weekly market. This was at a time when successive kings pursued an active policy of creating market towns as a new source of revenue. Some, owing to their more favourable locations, grew at the expense of others. Litcham was one of those which declined, so much so that by 1836 White observed that the market had long since been obsolete. Something of its former atmosphere is still embodied in the plan and fabric of the village, particularly Church Street. It was surely here that the market was held – that would explain the unusual width of the road and the elegance of the houses on the street.

From Priory Farm in the bottom of the Upper Nar Valley, the road climbs gradually uphill past the church and into the village centre which sits astride the B1145 at a point where several roads and country lanes converge. From most directions Litcham is approached across bleak, arable farmland, relieved only by stag-headed trees and occasional hedges. Dropping down into the village and the wooded valley bottom is refreshing. Here the spaces are closely defined by warm brick and flint cottages knitted together by garden walls, trees and conifer hedges. The contrast between these two environments is enhanced by some very well-defined edges to the village, unspoilt by ragged new development. Each main approach is marked by good individual or groups of buildings often strengthened by a backcloth of large mature trees.

This is particularly true of the road from Lexham. Cottages and outbuildings cluster before Litcham Hall, itself unusually near the road for such a notably Georgian building. The meadow opposite, however, is an integral part of the Hall's setting and it would be a shame to see it developed. As one approaches Litcham a magnificent beech by the roadside frames the view into the village.

The eastern edge is emphatic with a mass of trees in and around a disused chalk pit which has been included in the conservation area not only for its visual effect but also for its wildlife interest. Straight ahead at the crossroads stands a fanciful eighteenth-century cottage with an abundance of small pointed windows, heavy hood moulding and stepped gable.

The southern approach is quite different as alders, willows and the spread of the Warren punctuate valley-bottom meadows. Just across the river, Priory Farm has an impressive range of outbuildings as well as a tall eighteenth-century farmhouse marking the beginning of the village. The farm is unusual in that it incorporates the remains of a fourteenth-century hermitage. The result is a curious mixture of domestic red brick and ecclesiastical limestone embodied in projecting buttresses.

In contrast to the main east-west axis, Church Street is wide and impressive as it slopes downhill. It then sweeps round, narrows and continues towards

Above: *Church Street, Litcham, c.1935.*

Below: *Church Street, Litcham.*

Litcham village sign depicting Matthew Halcott.

Priory Farm. Not surprisingly the buildings here near the church are larger and more elegant eighteenth-century houses in red brick with pedimented doorways, tumbled gables and regular sash windows. These dwellings include the School House now crowded from behind by the new school buildings. Their massing, flat roof and drab red-brown brickwork strike a discord so close to the centre of the village. The church itself is set back from and a little above the road behind a tall, crowded row of trees. Its tower, which dates from 1699, is constructed from red brick and has little pinnacles. Inside there is a rood-screen with figure paintings said to date from 1436 and a fifteenth-century pulpit together with a west gallery dating from 1853.

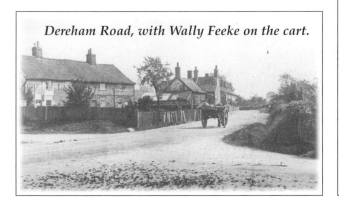

Dereham Road, with Wally Feeke on the cart.

COPY OF THE REVD A.E. BURTON'S NOTES ON THE LITCHAM CHARITIES

1. THE UNKNOWN DONOR'S CHARITY

This consists of the rents received from a field of about six acres on the Tittleshall Road divided into 66 gardens and 20 gardens on the fringe of the Common. The field was allotted to certain trustees by the Enclosure Act of 1760 in lieu of a number of small pieces of 'town land' all over the parish. The 'common gardens' were, by the permission of the lord of the manor, enclosed and cultivated by certain cottagers in the early part of the nineteenth century.

By a scheme of the Charity Commissioners, dated about 1900, these gardens, as well as the large field, are vested in and administered by a body of eight trustees, four of whom are permanent and four who are elected to serve for four years by the Parish Council. The four permanent trustees are in theory appointed by the Charity Commissioners, but in practice, when a vacancy occurs it is filled by a person elected by the surviving seven trustees. It was arranged from the beginning that the elected members retire two and two in alternate years, and those are the odd-numbered years (1951, 1953, etc.). The election should be at the first meeting of the Council of the year, usually in April. In case of a casual vacancy among the elected members, the Council fills it at once by electing a person to serve for the remainder of the term of the departed member.

From time immemorial the rents gathered by the trustees have been distributed as a dole per head of all parishioners of two years' standing who please to come for it at the time and place appointed (just before Christmas, master tradesmen excepted).

In about 1912 or 1913 the Charity Commissioners had the idea that such doles of money (about one shilling per head) were not good for people. They sent a Commissioner here to see what could be done in the way of applying the money in some better way. A parish meeting was held and the opposition to any change was unanimous and so strong that there was no chance of agreement. I then suggested that this was not strictly a charity; that the distribution was not the giving of a dole, but the paying of a dividend of the revenues of the parish property. The Commissioner accepted this way out of the difficulty and we heard no more of a proposed new scheme. (Perhaps the time is not far off when a change will be called for by the parishioners.)

2. THE ALLEE'S DOLE OR CHARITY

This was originally a sum of £2 a year for the poor, charged on certain land in Lexham. Mr Jessop redeemed this by payment to the Commissioners of a capital sum, which, invested at three per cent, produced

Mileham Road, Litcham, c.1900.

the £2 per year. Dalton, when Chancellor of the Exchequer, managed to reduce the rate of interest to two per cent so that the charity gets now only £1.13s.4d. This is paid in half-yearly installments by the Commissioners automatically into the trustee's account at Barclays Bank in East Dereham.

3. THE WODEHOUSE CHARITY

This is a sum of £3 a year for the poor, payable to trustees on 21 December, charged on part of the Litcham Manor Farm (Crane's).

Of late years the owner of the estate has instructed his bank to pay the sum on the proper date annually into the trustees account at Barclays Bank, East Dereham. But this instruction has several times been cancelled and the treasurer has been at the trouble of applying for payment. These two, Allee's and Wodehouse, are strictly charities for the poor. But for unnumbered years the two sums have been received by the trustees of the gardens and by them administered as part of their general income.

4. and 5. THE ALMSHOUSE AND GLOVER'S CHARITY

These are administered by a quite different body of trustees, viz. the rector (ex officio) and two persons elected for life by the Parish Council (J. Dent and O.J. Fisher). [N.B. In the original J. Dent has been deleted and the name of A. Fulcher added in pencil – D.F.N.] The house has four rooms, and there should be two inmates, each having an upper and a lower room. Each has also a small lean-to shed at the back. The Trust does not possess an inch of land outside the walls. The sole endowment is a charge of £2.10s. per quarter on High House Farm, Beeston (G. King). For many years it has been demanded and paid only once a year, that is £10 at Michaelmas.

Each inmate received £1 per quarter, so that after rates and insurance are paid there is little margin for repairs, etc. At present (1952) there is only one inmate. During the last ten or twelve years there has sometimes been none and it seems that in the future there may be no applicant for a vacancy. Thus a substantial balance has accumulated in the credit of the Trust.

There is sometimes some trouble about this £10 per annum. No owner of the farm has ever paid until he got a County Court summons and grumbled all the more because he had to pay the court fees in addition. But there has never been any trouble with the present owner. In paying he is entitled to deduct the income tax. But I have found it necessary to calculate this for him. Normally this is plain, but when the rate of tax is changed (in April) one has to calculate half a year at one rate and half a year at the other. But the payer must also give you a certificate on the proper form to the effect that he has deducted the tax. Then the treasurer fills in a certain form and sends it with that certificate to the income tax people and they refund the tax. There is no trouble with them. Each year when they send the cheque they send a form for the next year's claim. But they will not budge from this roundabout way of doing the business. (I used the last of my stock of the forms in 1951 but you can get a supply from the Tax Office.)

Church Street, Litcham, 1935.

Above: *Priory Bridge, Litcham, c.1930. Note The New Inn on the right which is no longer a village pub.*

Below: *Pound Lane, Litcham. The Green Dragon public house is on the right, 1920.*

*The Butter Market on the village green in East Lexham. Note the village sign standing on the bench in the centre.
This was bought by the village and the Foster family at the time of the Queen's Silver Jubilee. It was made by
Mr Carter of Swaffham.*

HISTORICAL LEXHAM

Lexham is a pleasant discovery for a stranger who, travelling from Norwich to King's Lynn, has the taste to take the B1145, winding its way through scattered villages and commons, in preference to the busy A47 trunk road. Even so, the stranger will not find Lexham unless he turns, a mile or so beyond the larger village of Litcham, on to a byway that forks to the left into a green tunnel of trees. Soon the woods on the left-hand side of the road open out to disclose a park with well-tended trees, cattle and an avenue leading to an elegant white house of the eighteenth century. Beyond the house is a lake fed by the upper stream of the little River Nar, which here is no more than a brook dammed into a series of small lakes.

Lexham Hall, the park and the lake are enclosed by woodland, except to the south where a broad avenue has been cut through the trees towards a vista of rolling West Norfolk farmland. The land, like the park, is notably well tended and intersected by good thorn hedges and long shelter-belts of mixed conifers and broad-leaved trees.

Several hundred yards past the Hall and its out-buildings you come to a little church with a round Saxon tower so rugged in construction that it is reminiscent of a North-Country peel tower. The church, standing against a background of trees, forms a beautiful group with the Elizabethan farm-house and the great flint-and-brick barn of Church Farm. Next to the farm lies the village of fewer than 150 inhabitants, its neat cottages spread around the green with a pretty little market cross, a village sign and a pond. Only in the light of closer knowledge does it become apparent that much of what the visitor sees today is the work of the last 30 years.

East Lexham is a very old village, the manor of which belonged to one Oschetel or Tokerel at the time of Edward the Confessor. The round flint tower of the church is said to date back to about the year AD850, and thus is one of the oldest buildings in the country that is still in use. After the Norman Conquest the Anglo-Saxon manor became one of the extensive properties of the great Earl William de Warrenne. The huge earthworks of his castle and the graceful ruins of the priory that he founded in 1085 survive at Castle Acre which is four miles away.

Lexham was passed down through the centuries to Stutevilles, Foliots, Hastings and L'Estranges, and then in 1585 to the Wodehouses of Kimberley in South Norfolk, who owned it for more than 200 years. It was probably Edmund Wodehouse (1649–1737) who built the earliest part of the present Lexham Hall. He bequeathed it to his nephew, Sir John Wodehouse, who built the larger and grander Kimberley House in 1720 but lived at Lexham until his death in 1754, leaving his son, Armine, to occupy Kimberley House. A second Sir John Wodehouse (created first Earl of Kimberley in 1797) enlarged Lexham Hall in 1780, but sold it in 1800. Six years later the Hall and estate were acquired by the Keppel family who lived there for another century, and further extended and altered the house during the Victorian era. Major Bertram Keppel sold Lexham in 1912 to Augustus Leverton Jessop, nephew to the Norfolk antiquary, Dr Augustus Jessop. Augustus Leverton Jessop died in 1932, but his widow, Laura, lived at the Hall until the war in surroundings that had hardly changed since the middle of the nineteenth century.

An early photograph of Lexham Road.

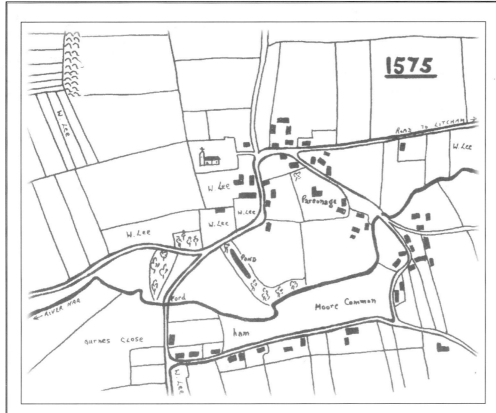

Left: *This map from 1575 shows the manor of Lord Phipps of West Lexham. It depicts 53 houses or buildings and a back lane close to the river. There were 18 farms in Lexham, mostly sited within separate tiny meadows, and the arable fields were subdivided into many narrow strips. Will Lee's meadows are marked here on the map; in addition he held 22 freehold strips and 16 'copie-hold' strips. Elizabeth Lee held another five strips. The parsonage was in the centre of the village.*

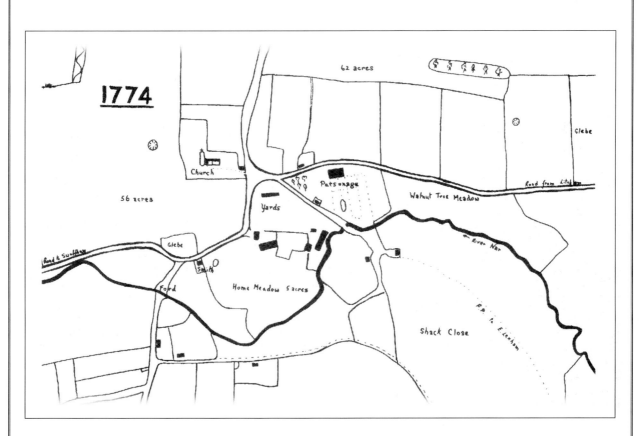

This map dates from 1774 and shows the village of Lexham four years after the Earl of Leicester had purchased the manor. There were then only 16 houses or buildings in the village and one farmyard near the church. This farm occupied all of the fields to the north, including Crowe Hall. A new parsonage had been built with a double-gable roof, a private fishpond and ornamental gardens. The present Lexham Manor was built in 1805, and many of the cottages in 1865, by the subsequent Earls of Leicester. The property was finally sold in 1943.

Mileham village sign depicting Mileham Castle.

HISTORICAL MILEHAM
(TAKEN FROM WHITE'S DIRECTORY
OF 1864)

Mileham is a long village of detached houses, two miles east-north-east of Litcham, and seven miles north-west of East Dereham, including within its parish 546 inhabitants, and 2,851 acres of land, mostly belonging to the Earl of Leicester, Capt. Davy, the Revd C.B. Barnwell, Mrs Barnwell and Mr E. Sparkes. The former is lord of the manor of Burghwood, but the Revd C.B. Barnwell is lord of the manors of Mileham and Beeston, and patron and incumbent of the rectory, which is valued at £11.1s.10d., and now has 16 acres of glebe, and a yearly tithe rent charge of £650, awarded in 1842. He resides at the Hall, a spacious red-brick building near the church, the rectory being in ruins.

The church (St John the Baptist) is furnished with neat poppy-headed benches; and comprises nave, aisles, chancel and square tower with four bells. The church land is 10 acres. Here was anciently a strong castle, built, as Blomefield images, by Alan, son of Flaad, to whom the Conqueror gave the manor. Some traces of the ditch and entrenchments, which occupied an oval area of 12 acres, may still be seen.

Mileham was the birthplace of that 'oracle of the law' Sir Edward Coke, who was son of Robert Coke, and was born in 1550, in the Old Hall, long since pulled down. Having been bred to the law, as his father had previously been, he so distinguished himself, as to rise to its highest honours and emoluments. In the early part of his career, he was first made recorder of Norwich, and then of London. He was afterwards appointed solicitor general to Queen Elizabeth, and speaker of the House of Commons; and subsequently became attorney-general, in which office he continued under King James, who successively appointed him Chief Justice of both benches. He died Lord Chief Justice of the King's Bench, 3 September 1634, aged 83. The learning of this eminent lawyer was at once profound, excursive and curious, and when he applied his strong mind to the illustration of a legal question he wholly exhausted the subject; and rather than quit, he would sometimes resort even to remote analogies. His works are still held in high esteem, and his commentary upon Littleton has become the 'bible of the law'. A sumptuous altar monument, bearing a Latin inscription, in the chancel of Tittleshall church, records his acquirements, honours and virtues.

The fuel allotment, awarded at the enclosure, in 1812, is 26 acres. The poor cut turf upon it and let the

The schoolhouse, The Street, Mileham.

herbage for about £20 a year, which is distributed in coals.

The national school, now attended by 70 children, was founded at an early period by Allan Elwyn, who gave the schoolroom, the master's house and garden, and about three acres of land. The present school was built in 1834.

In 1743, the Revd Chas Ward left £200 in trust to pay the interest of £50 to the schoolmaster, and to distribute the rest of the income, in six coats and gowns among six poor parishioners.

In 1773 the Revd Charles Barnwell charged his house, and 12 acres of land here, with the yearly payment of £5, for schooling four poor children.

Wm Glover, in the reign of Edward IV, gave four acres of land for the use of the church and poor. The latter have also the following yearly doles, viz. 3s.4d. left by Richard Thurrold, in 1628, out of land belonging to Capt. Davy (who generously distributes £5 yearly); about £3 as the interest of £100, left by Mary Barnwell, in 1780; and £5 left by Sarah Fewell in 1809, out of land now belonging to Mr Beeston, post from Swaffham.

Above: North View and a cottage which has since been demolished.

Right: Mr Dawes' machinery stored beside the charity coal-house where the village sign now stands.

Aerial view of Mileham showing the remains of Mileham Castle. This was anciently known as Arundel Castle and was built by the Fitzalan family, c.1100. The north side, north of the road, is the outer bailey and encompasses the present Burwood Hall built in 1973 on the site of the house where Sir Edward Coke was born. However, this may not be the site of the first Burwood Hall. Excavations in 1969 produced twelfth-century pottery. A selection of other pieces of medieval pottery, building materials and dead horses were found at various other dates and are now kept in Norwich Castle Museum. The base of the keep survives on the motte, used as an observer corps post during the Second World War. Large quantities of stone from the castle may have been used in rebuilding the church.

East Lexham, c.1910. Two men on horses returning from work.

Evacuees arriving at East Lexham, c.1940.

TWO

✣

PRINCIPAL BUILDINGS

There are numerous beautiful houses, farms and halls in Litcham, Lexham and Mileham, many of which date from the seventeenth and eighteenth centuries. The Litcham Historical & Amenity Society was formed partly due to the demolition of old buildings in the village and future plans for new development. Thankfully, a number of the buildings shown in the photographs in this chapter are now listed, thus preventing the villages from losing historically important properties in order to make way for new construction work.

The images in this chapter are a valuable record of dwellings and workplaces, some of which have disappeared altogether and others which have merely changed their function. It is important to maintain such archives for future generations.

Litcham Hall was built in the eighteenth century (possibly 1781) by Nicholas Raven. The Raven family were surgeons in Litcham in the nineteenth century and the Hall was nicknamed 'Pill Hall'. The Kypet family bought it at the beginning of 1900. It is now occupied by Mr and Mrs J.O.C. Birkbeck. It is a Grade II listed building.

Mileham Hall, one of several grand buildings which have been demolished.

West Lexham Hall is a Grade II listed building.

Priory Hermitage dates from the early-fourteenth century and is a Grade I listed building. It is a former chapel and hermitage which was used by pilgrims on their journey to Walsingham. The tanner of Litcham, Matthew Halcott, plied his trade here c.1610; he is featured on the village sign. Halcott also built the church tower in 1668/69 and was a great benefactor in Litcham.

The Post Office and general stores dates from the eighteenth century. It is both a shop and dwelling house and is Grade II listed. It once had dormer windows in the attic.

Above: *The corner shop was owned by the Rowe family who ran it as a hardware shop and cycle suppliers/repairers. The building is Grade II listed and dates from c.1860.*

Below: *The Bull Inn is a Grade II listed building which dates from the seventeenth century. The inn, which stands in the centre of the village, was originally thatched but now has a tiled roof. Court of Law was held in The Bull Inn until the late-eighteenth century.*

Above: *Canaan Row, Litcham.*

Below: *This is the dwelling adjoining the butcher's shop which is Grade II listed. The photo shows School House, formerly the harness-maker's house. At one time this was the butcher's home which had a slaughterhouse at the rear. Both buildings date from the eighteenth century.*

This Grade II listed building is Fourways which is a former toll-house dating from the nineteenth century. The last tolls, taken here in 1912, are recorded as 4d. for a horse and cart. Litcham's village museum (below, in 1998) is home to a large collection of photographs and artefacts relating to the local area.

Above: *Litcham Jubilee Hall, formerly the school, with All Saints Church visible to the right.*

Below: *The interior of Oddfellows Hall, Litcham, showing the decorations for the celebration of the Coronation of George V.*

The Green Dragon public house, Litcham, c.1909. The car in the photograph is a De-Dion.

Above: *Point House, Litcham, is Grade II listed and dates from 1830.*

Below: *Manor Farm is a late-sixteenth-century, Grade II listed building. This former farmhouse is situated opposite the church. Its upper storey was constructed from wattle and daub.*

Lexham Hall

BUILDINGS IN LEXHAM

When Lexham was purchased by W.R.B. Foster in the 1940s, the village and the estate were in a bad state of repair. Lexham Hall itself had been badly affected by the Second World War when a bomber had crashed in Saxon's Woods opposite the house causing damage to the windows. The estate had also been used as an RASC dump and parts of the house were used to shelter evacuees. Cottages and farms in the village were in a very bad state and it took many years of hard work to restore these dilapidated buildings to their current condition.

Left: *Church Farmhouse is a Grade II listed building. It is a former manor house dating from 1560 which was added to in the eighteenth century. The chimney is a nineteenth-century addition by Pugin.*

This photograph of Mileham shows Park Farm on the left; this is a Grade II listed dwelling which dates from the early-nineteenth century. Church Farm on the right is also Grade II listed and dates from the seventeenth century.

Burwood Hall in Mileham dates from 1793 and is a Grade II listed building.

Cottages in Rattle Row, Mileham. Those above are on the right heading down the lane and those below are on the left. Rattle Row eventually leads to the long-lost village of Grenstein. This village disappeared hundreds of years ago and is now remembered only by Grenstein Farm.

Mileham's old village hall (above) *and its more modern replacement* (below).

Mileham Post Office, 1950. The postmaster at this time was Mr Tomlin.

Bridge Farm, Beeston (now Litcham), c.1920. This is a fishery at the time of writing.

THREE
FAMILIES & LOCAL CHARACTERS

There are many individuals and families who have made an impact on Litcham, Lexham and Mileham. The photographs that follow in this chapter show these families living their daily lives, celebrate weddings and enjoy social gatherings. Individuals, couples and small groups are captured at work and at play. The people of the three villages are seen carrying out their trades, their leisure pursuits and their daily tasks.

These images preserve the faces and names of those who are no longer with us for the benefit of future generations.

Goddard family wedding photograph, also including members of the Yaxley, Collison and Archer families, 1962.

Above: *Middleage family wedding group, 1915.*

Below: *Banham family wedding group at Litcham Hall, 1920.*

Wedding group (the Wagg and Miles families), 1912.

Mr F. Fitt's wedding.

Above: *Photograph taken by Mr J. Melton, Litcham's photographer, of the Balderstone family.*

Below: *The Knock family, c.1900.*

The Robinson family, Mileham, 1880.

*Chemist Mr W. White with his wife and
family, 1900.*

Above: *The Waller family holiday in Great Yarmouth, c.1948.*

Right: *The Makins family, c.1920.*

Below: *E. Spencer and family, c.1912, with Model-T Ford.*

Above: *F. Fitt, F. Fitt senr, Anna Burton and Dian Fitt.*

Right: *The Rowe family, Corner Shop.*

Below: *The Fitt family and workers in the coalyard, c.1950.*

Above: *On top of the church tower, R. Maclellan, A. Lynn and A. Knock.*

Above: *Dr Dundas and family at The Mount, c.1900.*

Left: *Frank Claxton and Bob Hamilton.*

Above: *The Mann family and C. Collison.*

Below: *Mr and Mrs E. Goodings and family (The Bull Inn), 1958.*

Above: *Shopkeeper Mr Rowe and Dorothy Mann, riding the bike outside the Rowes' shop.*

Below: *Three 'old timers', Arthur Bush, Fred Fulcher and Freddy Linge.*

Some of the staff at Lexham Hall, c.1940. Second from the right is Mrs Lincoln and third from the right is Miss Jermy.

Dunham Station staff; Aubrey Thompson is on the right, c.1940.

Mr and Mrs Balderstone (Walter and May), c.1930.

Above: *Games in The Bull Inn, 1960. Pictured are: A. Collison, J. Fulcher and M. Mobbs.*

Below: *Mrs Burton, wife of Revd Burton who was rector at Litcham for 40 years, c.1910.*

Above: *Ethel and May Warnes, c.1918.*

LOCAL CHARACTERS

Walter Burton, 1910.

Above: *Mabel Burton, 1910.*

Mr E.T. Royle, 1950.

Edith King, c.1900.

Above: *George Mason, 1880.*

Right: *Edie Waller (with Cecil).*

Cyril Knock, 1940.

Sam Codling (butcher) in Hell Yard, 1914.

Driver J. Butcher of the Army Service Corps, 1914.

Above: *Dorothy Hardingham outside the bakery.*

Right: *J. Melton, Litcham photographer, c.1930.*

Above: *Abel Burton in Front Street, 1905.*

Below: *William Yaxley junr, c.1930.*

James Henry Knock, 1915.

Above: *Georgina Knock, 1920.*

Below: *Mrs D. Anthony in Post Office Yard (Symons paper room).*

Above: *Robert Moore, 1950.*

Above left: *James Knock, 1910.*

Above centre: *Maurice Smith, 1939.*

Above right: *Noan Neal, mole catcher, 1920.*

Right: *Mrs Askew, c.1910.*

John Feeke, c.1910.

Fred Fitt, 1930.

Lily Catton, 1929.

Arthur Howard (Oddfellows).

Above: *Mrs Twite, milk girl, c.1950.*

Below: *Mrs Lister, milkmaid at Chalk Farm, 1900.*

Above: *Mr A. Jessop Esq., lord of the manor, feeding pheasants in 1928.*

Below: *Mr Pigg ran the Post Office and general stores in Mileham.*

Above: *Abel Burton, 1905.*

Above: *E. Burton, Street Farm, Lexham, c.1910.*

Edith and Alfred Welch on an 1886 tandem.

Mr and Mrs G. Ramm with their horse and cart.

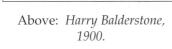

Above: *Mr and Mrs Middleton. Mr Middleton was village blacksmith for 52 years, c.1928.*

Right: *Billy Dixon, blacksmith at East Lexham for many years, c.1940s/50s.*

Below: *Dr and Mrs E. Knappett, 1950.*

Above: *Harry Balderstone, 1900.*

Above centre: *Mr and Mrs J. Waller.*

Below: *Mr and Mrs Syd Lome, Caanan Row Cottages, c.1950.*

Above: *Interior of The Limes, c.1900. Mr and Miss Lynes.*

Below: *Mr and Mrs Seaman of Lexham outside Laundry Cottage, 1882. Mr Seaman was noted for large pockets and a top hat. Both are buried in the churchyard.*

Left: *Abel and Hannah Burton. In her young days Mrs Burton is reputed to have been nanny to Lord Nelson.*

Right: *Joe and Edie Waller, c.1920.*

Above: *Mr and Mrs M. Mobbs, 1930.*

Below: *Mr and Mrs Patterson outside Fourways, c.1912.*

Below: *Mr and Mrs J. Oldfield in Back Street, c.1900.*

Above: *Wally Feeke with the honeycart, 1950. He is emptying the bucket in Mileham Road. It was said that when he went into the pub for a drink the bar was vacated rapidly!*

Road repairs in Church Street, 1925.

FOUR

VILLAGE TRADES & SERVICES

The coming of modern transport in the last 100 years and the rise of the supermarket in recent times have vastly altered the business communities of Litcham, Lexham and Mileham. Some 140 years ago most people lived all their lives in the villages and rarely ventured outside the immediate area. It was therefore necessary for the village to be self-sufficient.

In the twenty-first century, as in the past, the principal industry in this area is agriculture along with its many supporting trades. However, due to increased mechanisation, few people are needed to work on the land which has led to the disappearance of the localised support businesses. Tradesmen have suffered similarly as a result. Once the most vital mode of transport and work power, horses are now used only for sporting and pleasure purposes and the blacksmith in his forge, that old symbol of country life, has vanished along with the wheelwright and the saddler.

Dr and Mrs Highmoor at Waterloo House. Dr Highmoor practised in Litcham from 1901 to 1930.

Above: *Mr W. Yaxley, village carpenter, 1920.*

Above: *The blacksmith's house (the blacksmith was Christmas Burgess), 1930.*

Left: *Ben Howard was a local craftsman. He used the osier-beds on the Common for basket making, c.1920.*

Below: *James Parker Mitchell, wheelwright, 1900. Photograph by Litcham's local photographer, J. Melton.*

Bottom: *The wheelwrighting workshop in Pound Lane, Litcham.*

Right: *Mr A.*
Rowe was the
shopkeeper at
the cycle shop.

Above and right: *Mr and Mrs*
E. Spurgeon, shopkeepers, 1900.

Below: *Mr Symonds 'Bruiser',*
cobbler and shopkeeper.

Above: *Mileham shop, 1941.*

Below: *Mileham shop, June 2002.*

Above: *Butchers, 1920. Left to right: Miss Anstee, G. Mitchell, J. Goodings, N. Scott, H. Lincoln.*

Left: *Mr Archer, Wendling butcher, 1910.*

George Catton, butcher, 1920.

Above: *Mr Jack Fulcher, butcher's roundsman, 1935.*

Below: *Mr Rogers with Mrs E. Howe, grocer's delivery, c.1930.*

Among the many Mileham shops that have closed are the three bakers, the last of which ended its long service in 1994 – much to the dismay of residents who had long enjoyed 'real' bread. These photographs show the last baking at the village bakery which was owned by the Minster family at the time of its closure in 1994.

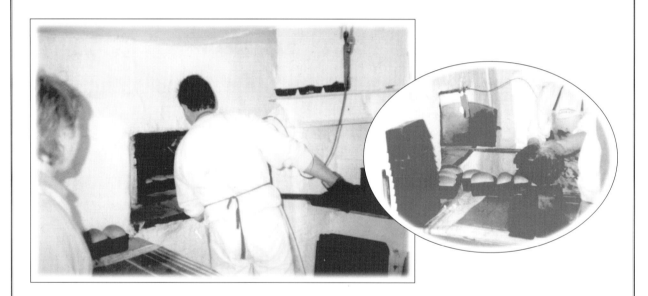

∽ THE LIMEKILNS ∽

Left and below: *The Grade II listed limekilns played a significant role in employment in Litcham over 100 years. One limekiln is now restored and it is possible to view it. These photographs show the kilns in use at the beginning of the 1900s.*

Corners Garage, Front Street, c.1930.

Above: *Carter's Coaches, c.1949. Director Gordon Carter.*

Left: *Gordon Carter (Carter's Coaches), 1940.*

Right: *Bessie Carter (Carter's Coaches), 1940.*

Left: *C.W. Bell & Son started life in Mileham in roughly 1931 with one seven-ton lorry stored at Hall Farm, Mileham, under the name of Bell & Rye. The partnership was dissolved in the late 1950s and the company then started to trade under the name of C.W. Bell. In the 1970s the business became C.W. Bell & Son and, at the time of writing, operates up to ten 44-ton tractor units and trailers under this name. Mr P.A. Bell runs the business from its premises in Mileham.*

Below: Mr Sizeland's wood yard in Back Lane.

Lexham Hall

English Table Wine

Muller Thurgau Vintage 1979

70 cl

Estate Bottled and Produced by W.R.B. Foster, Lexham Hall, Kings Lynn, Norfolk, UK

A label taken from a bottle of wine produced at Lexham Hall during the latter half of the twentieth century.

VILLAGE PUBS

There were three licensed premises in Mileham during the nineteenth century, The Castle, The Unicorn and The Oak. These pubs have now all disappeared, with the final closure of The Oak in 1989, and in 2002 thirsty villagers have to travel more than a mile into Litcham to find a local!

East Lexham once had a pub called The Chequers which was closed c.1955/6 and converted into a village clubhouse; this in turn was later made into two houses. West Lexham had a pub called The Red Lion which is no longer there. There are no shops in Lexham. The Lexham Hall wine label was started in 1975 by N.W.D. Foster who planted a vineyard on the estate. Despite producing large quantities of wine for several years, the vineyard no longer exists. The image above is a label from one of the bottles of wine produced there.

Until fairly recently, Litcham boasted several pubs. There was The Green Dragon, The New Inn and The Kings Arms but, at the time of writing, there is only The Bull Inn.

Above: *Mr and Mrs Goodings in the yard of The Bull Inn.*
The Goodings family ran the inn for two generations.

Right: *Post Office yard, Webtale and C. Elliot.*

Above: *Mr Warnes, postman, 1960.*

Below: *Mrs Brenda Woods, postwoman, delivering post to Mrs Bell with young D. Lynn, 1950.*

Above: *Police Constable Waters, 1950.*

Above: *Sergeant Bush with his bicycle, 1925.*

Below: *Litcham Fire Brigade winning the cup, 1939.* Left to right: *A. Knock, K. Ewen, F. Riches, B. Benshaw, A. Fulcher, B. Fitt, E. Harris.*

Above: *Police Sergeant and Constable, old police house, Shadrack Cottage, 1912.*

Left: *Litcham's last local policeman, PC D. Stuart (left), receiving his long-service medal. He left his position c.1990.*

Right: *Litcham Police Station once nestled between these houses, these are now two separate dwellings.*

A corn-mill was recorded in Mileham as early as 1675. By 1775 a post-mill was on the same site and a tower-mill was built adjacent to it, probably in the 1840s. By 1898 the tower-mill was dilapidated and the post-mill derelict. The mill was restored by John Wilkin and in 1902 was back in working order with a 'tarred tower, white cap and sails and a scarlet fan'. Work was continued until 1918 and the mill was finally dismantled in 1937; all that remains today is the ivy-covered tower. The photograph shows Mileham corn-mill before it was terminally damaged by a storm in 1918.

FIVE

❧

FARMING & AGRICULTURE

Today, as in the past, the principal industry in the rural Breckland region is agriculture with its many supporting trades, yet the employment that this provides is diminishing as fewer people are needed to work on the land.

In farming, horsepower has been replaced by machinery and thus the photographs in this chapter serve more as a reminder of days gone by than as a reflection of the agricultural living that is now made on the local farms.

These images capture villagers as they work hard on the land; they are seen picking crops, harvesting, cultivating and tending for the parkland. They also show those people who go hand in hand with agriculture, the gamekeepers, the estate-workers and the gardeners.

THE AGE OF STEAM

Above: *Steam traction engines were an important piece of equipment on farms in the 1920s.*
Left to right: *Alec Ward, Aubrey Walpole, Willow Walpole, Wilby Dye, A. Dawes, Mr Butler and George Burrell. The two men on the engine are Bussie Prior and 'Blue' Webster.*

Above: *Steam engine auction (Burton), 1930.*

Below: *Ploughing with a steam engine. Robert Egleton is holding the oil can.*

Above: *Model traction engine made by Mr Dawes (pictured) who owned a haulage and threshing business.*

Below: *Spencers steam engine.*

Above: *Billy Neale (Twigham), c.1920.*

Below: *Seed drilling.*

Above: *T. Twite at Oaklands Farm, 1947.*

Below: *Group on Manor Farm, c.1920.*

Bob England, a farmworker at Park Farm, Mileham, c.1920.

Above and right: *Harvest at Kempstone, c.1900.*

Below: *Threshing at Kempstone, 1925.*

Above: *Drain laying, 1922. Included are: R. Thompson, E. Goff, ? Twite, R. Wagg.*

Below: *The Cresswell family at Chalk Farm, c.1900.*

Above: *A. Twite at Oaklands Farm, 1950.*

Below: *Oaklands Farm, c.1950.*

Above: *Lexham estate workers, 1960. Jack Creed, Albert Lister, Alfred Fulcher, Charlie Bodimeade, Robert Green, Billy Clarke, David Bambridge, Lloyd Askew, Ted Hewitt.*

Right: *Walter and Tom Smith and Charlie Dodman at Kempstone.*

Below: *Threshing on Lexham Road, c.1940.*

Above: *Gamekeepers in Pound Lane, 1920.*

Below: *Gamekeepers from East Lexham.*

Above: *Grass cutting, c.1900. Mr Moore and Mr Calaby.*

Right: *Eustace Goodings and Albert Collison.*

Below: *A more modern scene – liming in 1962. It is interesting to note how much more sophisticated machinery has become in the last 60 years.*

Litcham Common.

Working party on Litcham Common, 1950. Included are: A. Smith, J. Udal, W. Coleman, C. Coleman.

All Saints Church, Litcham.

Six
Churches & Chapels

All Saints Church, Litcham

There is no remaining trace of the Anglo-Saxon pre-Conquest church which would have stood on the site of the present building; nor of the Norman church which followed it. In 1397 the lord of the manor had a grant for a fair to be held yearly on All Saints Day, which is the dedication festival of the church (1 November).

It is conjectured that the church fell into a semi-ruinous state during the period of the Black Death (1348–9 and 1369) and was largely rebuilt and probably enlarged during the period of economic recovery after that. It was re-consecrated on the Feast of St Botolph, 17 June 1412, and the 550th anniversary of this event was observed in 1962. There was a bel-fry with three bells in the west wall until the seventeenth century when Matthew Halcott, a wealthy tanner, gave the present brick tower in 1669. There are signs that the thatched roof, destroyed by a fire which swept through the village in 1636, was replaced by a roof of steeper pitch than the present slate one. Records show that the roof was still thatched in 1825. The church clock is by Morris of Swaffham, given by the rector, the Revd Peter Smyth, in 1750. There are now six bells in full working order.

The present porch was constructed from older pews and the wooden ceiling made up out of former Ten Commandment boards on which some of the lettering is still visible. In the porch is an alms box carved out of solid oak and iron-bound with three locks.

THE LITCHAM CRYPTOGRAM

The Litcham cryptogram is engraved on the middle pillar on the south side of the nave. A suggested interpretation of the cryptogram is:

'Save (my soul) Jesus, Mary and Joseph. The Manifestum *or (maybe)* Memento Mori, *of Wyke Bamburgh.'*

The interior of All Saints Church, Litcham.

As one stands in the south aisle, a glance around the nave is sufficient to show that the building has many features of unusual artistic delicacy. The piers of the nave have the most beautiful slender shafts, the hood mouldings of the arches terminating in human heads with wavy hair and pointed beards. These act as label stops between the arcade arches and are designed to fit the space exactly. One also notes the mouldings where the chancel arch meets the arcade, and the most unusual mouldings and window tracery.

A curious and as yet unexplained feature of All Saints Church is the 'odd' pillar in the south-west aisle. It is octagonal and rests on a square base of stone which probably dates from an earlier period. It is suggested that this may be all that is left of an earlier arcade, perhaps in an earlier building. The arch does not rest centrally over the column. The piers, arches and mullions of the windows in the church are rich in masons' marks and the window in the west wall, partly hidden by the organ in the gallery, is of an earlier period (c.1307–27).

The name of the master builder responsible for Litcham church is not reliably known, though following C.G. Coulton (*Art and the Reformation*), Dr E. Puddy in his book on Litcham attributes this to William Hindley, later master at Norwich Cathedral (the Erpingham Gate) and York Minster (choir screen). The tracery design of the perp windows follows a rare pattern which is found at Carbrooke and Lynn St Nicholas, and is part of the 1412 restoration of the church.

In the south aisle there is a defaced Holy Water stoup which was revealed in 1965. At about eye-level on the middle pillar on the south side of the nave is what is known as the Litcham cryptogram, probably a pilgrim's prayer (Litcham was the final halt on the road from London to the shrine of Walsingham) scratched in the hard chalk or 'clunch' of the pillar. A suggested interpretation is 'Save (my soul) Jesus, Mary and Joseph. The *Manifestum* or (maybe) *Memento mori*, of Wyke Bamburgh.'

In the south-east corner of the aisle is a medieval piscina, revealed also by the Revd N. Newns in 1965 which is of the most exquisite craftsmanship. There were formerly three medieval trade guilds, of All Saints, of St John the Baptist, and of the Resurrection, each with its own chapel, one in the nave, where the present altar table now stands, and the other two at the east end of the aisles. A fourth guild, that of St Anne, is mentioned in a will. There are slots cut in the bases of the easternmost pillars for the reception of screens to these side chapels. The only glass remaining of the medieval stained glass is fragmentary in the tracery of the window nearest the pulpit. Four tiny angels in the tracery look downwards, pointing to the main lights which must have contained more figures; it is possible to see, through binoculars, a forked beard amongst the fragments arranged at the top. In the next window there is a modern stained-glass memorial to Ken Sharples who, as church treasurer, played a leading part in restoring the windows of this church.

The chancel rood-screen is undoubtedly the glory of Litcham church. It dates from 1436 and was carefully restored (except for the panel paintings) in 1901; with its doors still intact it is an unusual feature. The theme of the rood-screen is the saints, with females on the north side and males on the south, there being 22 paintings in all. The upper portion of the screen has five ogee arches with exquisite tracery which are cusped and doubly feathered and the centre arch is of double width. The only decipherable panel on the doors is the southernmost one on which can be seen three black money bags hanging from the girdle of St Nicholas. The chancel is structurally separate from the nave and strangely plain in comparison to its beauty. Its windows appear to be of the same period as the west window, the frames being made from the original clunch, but the mullions, though similar in design, appear to be modern replacements.

The beautifully carved Litcham coffer, dating from the 1300s, stands in the chancel and is one of only five oak chests in England that is of Flemish craftsmanship. In the sanctuary stands a stall which is double seated with carved misereres. All of the heads have been defaced but if the seat is tipped up one can see a face with a forked beard. This probably dates from about the time of the 1412 restoration. In the vestry, on the site of an earlier chapel or vestry, is a squint in the north wall of the chancel which provides a view of the altar table. Inside is a framed plan of all the monumental floor slabs in the church.

The pulpit dates from the fifteenth century, it is hexagonal with Perpendicular panels and it rests on a slender wineglass stem. The pulpit was bought in a London junk shop in 1890 and given to the church by the Revd W.A.W. Keppel. It still shows slight traces of what may have been medieval colouring. At the time of writing, the supports for the pulpit handrail are four fluted columns which were once supports for the flat baseboard of the font cover. The font has an octagonal bowl in Perpendicular style with six foil panels enclosing plain suspended shields. The bowl is lead-lined with indents for the reception of padlocks which would have secured the cover in medieval times. In 1840 the font had a huge canopy above it.

The western gallery of the church has moulded metal tracery; the original carving from which the moulds were cast now serves as a notice-board on the left-hand side of the inner doorway of the porch.

Above: *The rood-screen in Litcham church.*

Below: *Litcham's fourteenth-century country church coffer.*

THE CHURCH OF ST ANDREW, EAST LEXHAM

The Church of St Andrew in East Lexham, which dates from around AD900, is reputed to be the oldest round tower in the country. Buildings that have been in continuous use for that span of time must be exceedingly rare. The shape of the church tower is crudely circular and it tapers on the outside at belfry level. Despite having been capped with an octagonal roof, the appearance of the church has been altered remarkably little from its original state. The flints from which the building is constructed are laid in courses with occasional bands of larger flints. Between these a substantial amount of mortar was used, suggesting that there were large intervals during construction in order to allow it to set. It may well have taken several seasons to build the tower.

There are three belfry openings in the church in place of the usual four. The south-west belfry opening is constructed entirely from flints and has a round-headed arch. Within this arch two round-headed lights are set back on the jambs and are supported in the centre by a typical Saxon baluster made from flints and coated with plaster. It has a special stone for its capital which was probably an

erratic found locally. The north-west belfry opening is a single stone cut to match the south-west one. The east-facing one is unique in that is has a Maltese cross carved from stone which is set within a stone frame.

The lancet window in the ground floor of the tower was added during the fourteenth-century early-English period. From inside the tower there is some evidence of a ring of circular openings above the belfry. The bell is an early one with a latin

 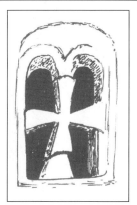

East Lexham church belfry openings. The east-facing belfry opening is unique in that it is carved to the shape of a Maltese cross within a stone frame (above right).

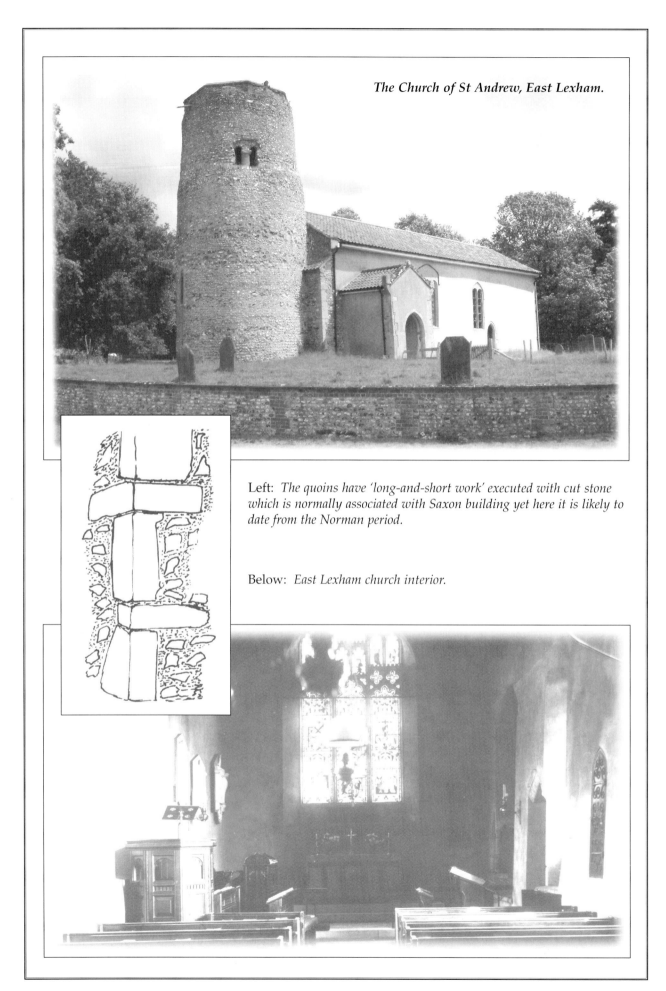

The Church of St Andrew, East Lexham.

Left: *The quoins have 'long-and-short work' executed with cut stone which is normally associated with Saxon building yet here it is likely to date from the Norman period.*

Below: *East Lexham church interior.*

Above: The rood-loft stairs have been converted into a book cupboard. The door is decorated with intricate ironwork.

inscription in Gothic miniscules; when translated the inscription reads, 'I am called the bell of Virgin exalted Mary.' It was probably cast by Brasyer in the fifteenth century. The triangular-headed upper doorway on the first floor would have had a wooden ladder or staircase for access from the nave. This arrangement saved losing valuable floor space within the tower and there were no benches in the nave at the time when the doorway was in use. The walls of the church are continuous throughout the nave and chancel and it is likely that they are Saxon in origin although none of the windows are particularly old. There is no chancel arch in St Andrew's Church.

The quoins all have 'long-and-short work' executed with cut stone. This is normally associated with Saxon buildings but here it is more likely that it was done as repair during the Norman period when such stones became available. One would expect that there were flint corners at first but this is a poor material for such construction, although there were no alternatives locally during the Saxon period.

The porch contains a stone coffin lid in the floor and an early-English doorway. The north doorway is blocked and the space is used for a war memorial

which is brightly painted with the figure of St Michael driving out evil in the form of a dragon and at the same time holding scales weighing the souls of the just and the unjust. The royal arms on the west wall were painted for George IV (1816–37). The Commandment boards are also seen there. The font is Victorian and decorated with conventional flowers and arches.

The rood-loft stairs were in the thickness of the south wall. They have been converted into a book cupboard with a fine door which has decorative ironwork. The angel piscina in the chancel is a beautiful feature dating from the Perpendicular period. It has an ogee arch on one side and a half-round arch on the other side. Both have cinquefoil cusping and are supported by round shafts with stilted bases. It is believed that the misericords in the church came from Castle Acre Priory at the time of the Dissolution of the Monasteries in 1537.

The east window has early-Victorian stained glass, probably by Clayton and Bell, c.1859. It is a good design in the manner of fifteenth-century Norwich work and has a great variety of colours. Across the bottom of the window the picture panels illustrate the Annunciation, the Nativity and the Presentation of Christ in the temple. The Crucifixion is in the centre flanked by Christ carrying his Cross and the Deposition. At the apex we see angels announcing that 'He is risen' with two soldiers asleep at the tomb. On each side of this are witnesses of the Resurrection, St Peter and St John on one side and the three women bearing spices on the other.

The churchyard is roughly circular and surrounded by a ditch. The church stands on a slight mound which suggests that this was once a site for pagan worship and that when the people were converted to Christianity in the seventh century, a Christian church was planted on the site to finally put an end to the pagan activities. When the churchyard wall was rebuilt the skeleton of a young man was found;

he had been shot through the head with a musket. The site of the Saxon village was north-east of the church where trees grow now.

Left: The angel piscina in the chancel has an ogee arch on one side and a half-round arch on the other.

Left: *War memorial in East Lexham church.*

Below: *The carving of a donkey on the alms box at West Lexham church. This box was given in memory of George Palmer who was a churchwarden and estate carpenter for 30 years.*

THE CHURCH OF ST NICHOLAS, WEST LEXHAM

The site of the Church of St Nicholas is evocative, with the dwellings by the river and the church on its hill alongside. The churchyard is suggestive of a circular pre-Christian hilltop site on an escarpment. Here the glaciers of the Ice Age melted and deposited a moraine of stones; pine trees have been planted where the soil was not good enough to cultivate. The pines on the north side of the church were planted in 1965 and are called the Churchill Plantation. The round tower has survived some very bad times and undergone desperate restoration work to save it. Although without doubt a Saxon tower of the eleventh century it has lost some of its Saxon features. The thickness of the tower walls is two feet, six inches, which is significant because during the Norman period such walls were made over three feet thick. The D-shape of the tower indicates that it was added onto an existing church wall; the part above the west wall of the nave was reconstructed with bricks in 1881. The irregular shape of the tower throughout suggests that it was built by inexperienced men with inadequate materials. A hard chalk, 'clunch', was used with the local flints and lime mortar to construct the walls and this can be seen inside the belfry. Feltwell's round tower also used clunch in this manner but it fell down.

The triangular-headed window frames on the ground floor face both north and south and were made by leaning together a pair of clunch stones in the simple manner used prior to the Norman Conquest. This is best seen on the north side. The clunch stones are now badly weathered and the windows were blocked up with flints when the tall west-facing lancet was opened in the fourteenth century. The four belfry openings are not original; they are fourteenth-century insertions and are set on the diagonals (i.e. south-east, south-west, north-west and north-east). There is a parapet with sloping bricks at the rim of the round tower, and the roof and parapet are made almost invisible by the convex curve of the surrounding ground. The tower roof is tiled to an apex within the parapet and has brick arches at each end, below which there is visible a nineteenth-century brick arch which carries the weight of the roof. In the 1820s Robert Ladbrooke drew this church with a pyramidal roof and a weather vane.

There was a major restoration in 1881 which involved much rebuilding of the nave and chancel by the rector, the Revd F.F. Reavely, in memory of his wife who laid the foundation stone three months before her death. This is recorded on a large plaque inside the chancel. A drawing which hangs in the church is Dr Puddy's copy of a sketch which was done when the rebuilding was in progress. There is no record of any disaster at that time, so it seems more likely that the rebuilding was completed out of enthusiasm for making the church perfect after a period of neglect. Records include a complete list of rectors from 1339 to the present day.

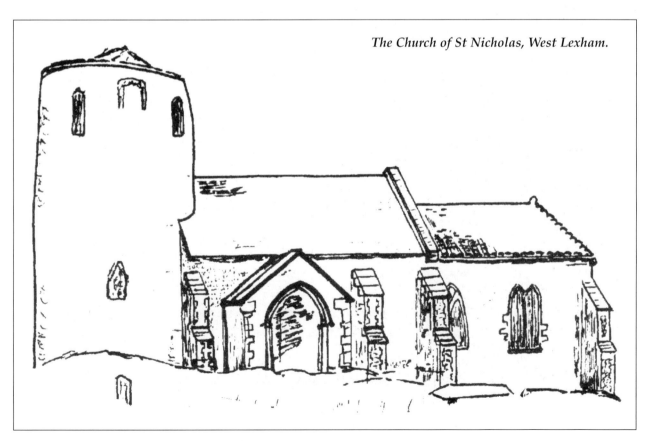

The Church of St Nicholas, West Lexham.

The churches at East and West (above) Lexham are fine examples of Saxon round-tower churches.

Above: The diamond-shaped Italian marble floor tiles in the sanctuary were given as a gift by the second Earl of Leicester.

In 1993 the tower had a number of desperate cracks and threatened to collapse like the round tower at Onehouse in Suffolk. Stainless steel stitches were inserted in the masonry overlapping one another and encircling the tower at various levels. Following that the whole surface was re-plastered. It is thought that this tower always had a lime plaster finish on the outside to protect the clunch.

A stone coffin lid inside the tower is probably that of a priest from the thirteenth century; it has a Celtic-type cross at the head end and a double omega pattern. The chancel arch has double hollow chamfers and demi-octagonal capitals typical of the early-fourteenth century. There are marks on the columns where the chancel screen used to fit. The walls of the nave and chancel are continuous throughout, which is a feature shared by many early churches, including the one at East Lexham.

Italian marble tiles in fine diamond shapes and three colours make up the floor of the sanctuary; they were the gift of the second Earl of Leicester at the time of the Victorian restoration. He was the landowner and his tenant lived in the Hall. The east

window glazing was signed by L. Lobin of Tours in 1882, a French glazier using a style here that was favoured in England 30 years earlier. It shows the Risen Christ giving His blessing and it is surrounded by colourful medallions with scenes of the Nativity, Christ's Presentation in the temple, Emmaus, the Resurrection and the Angel at the empty tomb. The picture of the boy Jesus (on show inside the church), illustrates Luke 2.46, when He had come straight from His home village at the age of 12 to debate with the doctors of law in the temple in Jerusalem, and 'all that heard Him were astonished at His understanding and answers.' This is copied from part of a much larger picture which includes all of the scribes around Him and is appropriate to this friendly village church where so many generations of village people have worshiped Jesus. The alms box has a fine carving of a donkey and was given in memory of George Palmer who was a churchwarden and estate carpenter for 30 years.

THE CHURCH OF ST JOHN THE BAPTIST, MILEHAM

The fabric of the Church of St John the Baptist tells something of the history of this place, its people and their worship over the past eight centuries. There was a church on this site long before that when the Saxon village was positioned to the south. Stigand was lord of the manor at Mileham when he became Bishop of Elmham in 1043 and then, because he was Archbishop of Canterbury at the time of the Conquest in 1066, his manor was taken over by the Normans and a motte-and-bailey castle built here.

Above: Former head of Mileham School, Mr Howard, playing Mileham church organ.

The Church of St John the Baptist, Mileham.

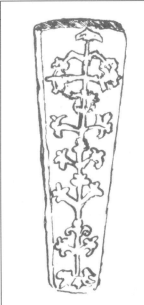

Top: *Sketch of the Church of St John the Baptist, Mileham.*

Above: *A sketch of one of the large stone coffin lids reset beside the north and south doors of the church. They are decorated with a foliated cross and symbols of eternity.*

Left: *The alms box is made out of solid oak and has three locks.*

The church is famous for its west window which has the beautiful double-reticulated tracery of the Decorated period. This still contains much of its original stained glass dating from about 1340. This was given by the patron, Lord Richard Fitzalan, to mark his marriage into the royal family of Lancaster. He then went to fight in the Battle of Crecy (1346) and on returning victorious he inherited a great fortune from his wife's uncle and added the tower to the church. The tower is set on the north side of the church where it serves as a porch and not where it might cast a shadow on the donor's wedding window. The parapet was added to the tower as a result of a legacy from Richard Scarlet in 1457. The knapped white flints show up from the more distant parts of the parish. On the top corners are seated figures of Matthew, Mark, Luke and John. The church has five great bells which were cast in 1877 by Mears, the ringing of which cracked the tower from top to bottom. The date 1974 is scratched on the internal plaster to mark where the cracks were stitched and filled. The clock, which chimes on the tenor bell, came to Mileham church from West Tofts church at some time around 1850 and was already considered to be an antique then.

The roof of the nave was constructed in 1882 by William Curtis, a Litcham builder, using Westmoreland slates. The chancel roof was rebuilt about the same time but with Welsh slates. This reminds us that in those days the chancel was kept by the rector. It took six years for the parish to complete

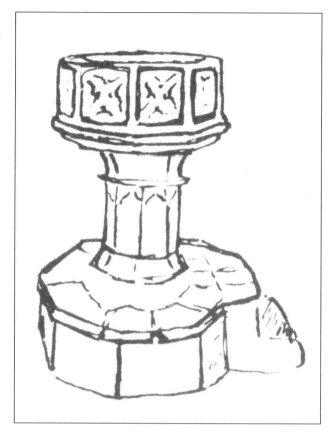

Above and below: *The font in Mileham church which has quatrefoils on seven of its eight sides, indicating that it was made to stand against a wall or pillar.*

payment for the nave roof. Inside, at the corners of the roof, medieval corbel heads of a man with a forked beard, possibly St John the Baptist, can be seen. The angel corbels are Victorian as well as the box pews on which earlier poppy-heads have been reset. A bench at the back of the south aisle survives to show us how the church was furnished previously.

The font has quatrefoils on seven out of eight sides which indicates that it was made to stand against a wall or square pillar. It probably occupied the place near the main entrance where the alms box stands at the time of writing, which demonstrates the significance of baptism being the point at which one enters the church. The previous font bowl was found in the garden of Burwood Hall and returned to the back of the church. The alms box was made out of solid oak with three locks so that the rector and both churchwardens had to be present to open it. Judging by the space inside, coins were small and valuable in those times. There are large stone coffin lids reset beside the north and south doors which are decorated by a foliated cross and symbols of eternity. One can only speculate whether they belonged to priests or early builders of the church.

The arcading on the north side of the church is based on massive crude rectangular piers which some authorities suggest are earlier than those on the south side. But with both round and octagonal designs on that side it seems possible that the builders ran into structural difficulties with the more elegant piers and changed to stronger designs as they progressed. The south aisle arcading leans outwards in an alarming manner and the clerestory wall bulges also. It was strengthened by a thorough restoration in 1981 which transferred the thrust to massive reinforced concrete bases underground. There are now L-shaped beams at each end of the aisle and two steel beams across the aisle to buttresses which conceal further reinforced concrete beams.

The east window of the south aisle has beautiful flowing tracery of the Decorated period, c.1340, and there is still much of the roof timber of that age to be seen including some lovely designs of wood-carving in the spandrels. The south windows date from about 100 years later and the top of one of these Perpendicular-period windows encroaches on the wall-plate timber, suggesting that the carpentry here is original fourteenth century. There is attractive internal shafting which is not present in the north aisle. The pulpit is pre-Reformation with a wineglass stem and has been restored more than once. The angle of the hymn board demonstrates the leaning wall. Above the pulpit there is an irregularity in the wall and it seems likely that an earlier chancel arch was sited about three feet west of the present Perpendicular-period arch. There is a chancel south window of c.1300–10 which is now unreasonably close to the present chancel arch. The

The altar tomb at the entrance to the churchyard is the subject of much speculation. Its design suggests that a nobleman, possibly a keeper of the castle, might have improved the church.

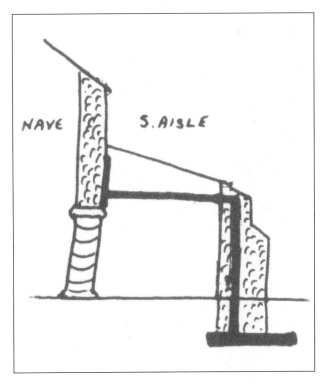

A diagram showing the lean of the arcading in the south aisle. The black lines show the reinforced concrete bases that were installed during restoration work in 1981.

brass in the floor of the south aisle portrays Christopher Crowe and his wife, Christian, with their children in two panels below. This is a London-made brass with its inscription in abbreviated English. Christopher Crowe died in 1526 and it is wondered whether he was related to Nicholas Crowe who was rector in 1542.

The upper half of the west window is all eleventh-century stained glass with lovely deep greens and browns. In the centre is St John the Baptist with brown legs holding the Agnus Dei; he is flanked by St Catherine and St Margaret. The canopy work above them is most elaborate but the portrayal of perspective is not good, confirming its early date of c.1340. Three panels of paler glass in the lower half are works from the fifteenth century and have been moved from other windows in the church. It seems likely that their position was occupied by heraldry in the original composition which may have been removed during the Wars of the Roses. Further fragments at the bottom of the window include some very early roundels. This window is the largest surviving example of fourteenth-century glass in Norfolk and, according to local tradition, it was saved from destruction by having many coats of whitewash over it.

The chancel once had a priest's door with Norman shafting and a pointed arch above; this was blocked up at the time of the Victorian restoration when the sanctuary floor was raised and re-paved with tiles. The doorway has a scratch dial on the outside and is the earliest identifiable feature of this church. The pointed arch above the cushion capitals could indicate a date from around 1200 when the Norman style was changing to the early-English period, or it could be an early modification. A round window high up on the north side of the chancel has been plastered over for centuries but is now visible from the outside and could be from the same period as the doorway.

On each side of the chancel's east window were elaborate fifteenth-century niches for statues of saints. These were crudely chipped off so that Commandment boards could be fixed over them. Then, at the time of the Victorian re-roofing, the boards were removed to allow iron tie-bars to strengthen the outer corners. Prominent in the chancel are memorials to the Barnwell family. The ledger slabs have particularly fine heraldry deeply incised and the wall monuments are classical in style. Barnwells were patrons here for 250 years and lived in Mileham Hall which was totally demolished in 1947. Near the communion rail there is a ledger slab to Fermor Pepys, cousin of the diarist; it gives a fine description of his exemplary life. On the other side is a slab commemorating the children of Thomas Browne who all sadly died in infancy – it gives the dates of their birth, baptism and burial.

The south-east window of the chancel contains a panel of stained glass showing two kneeling figures in blue behind a paniered pony and the name of Thomas Broun. These are donors of a window in the Perpendicular period. Referring to the list of rectors there was David Brown 1443–47, so one may speculate whether this might refer to his parents.

The altar tomb bearing a fine cross is sited near the entrance to the churchyard and is also the subject of much speculation. The tomb bears shields with lancer's slots set within quatrefoils which suggest that some great nobleman like Richard de Burwood or Sir John Cornwall, keepers of the castle, might have improved the church. The shaft of the cross is decorated with four pretty little niches, weathered over many centuries. This building has been the place of prayer for the people of Mileham for eight centuries and tells us something of how each generation has contributed to it.

Left: The priest's door that was blocked up at the time of the Victorian restoration.

THE CHAPELS IN THE THREE VILLAGES

There were three Nonconformist chapels in Litcham, the first being the Primitive Methodist Chapel built in 1832 in Bull or Butt Lane. This chapel remained in use until 1948 when it was sold, the roof having fallen into a serious state of disrepair. The diverse elements of the Free churches are evident from the fact that the Wesleyans built their own chapel in Back Street in 1846. This building remained in use until the time of the First World War and was later used as a garage. It was demolished some years ago, as were the shop and other buildings on the green and no evidence of its existence now remains, although the pulpit was removed to the chapel in Front Street. The third chapel, the only one which is still in use in any of the three villages at the time of writing, came about due to the amalgamation of some of the other elements of the Free churches. Building commenced in Front Street in 1909.

In 1932 the various sections of Methodism in this country were mostly united, forming what is now the Methodist Church. The effect of this union of the Free churches in Litcham led eventually to worship being centred in the chapel in Front Street and the end of the other two chapels. Primitive Methodism was introduced into East Lexham in 1836. The original meeting-place was in a cottage, followed by a hired building. In due course a chapel was built in

The Street; no trace of this building now remains. The following is an extract from the 'Primitive Methodist Church Centenary Celebrations, Souvenir of the Swaffham Circuit 1836–1897', in the possession of Mr Norman Wagg:

East Lexham is situated in a valley, and its moral condition has resembled Ezekial's valley of dry bones. But lately the winds of the spirit have blown upon them, and they are beginning to live. Seven or eight souls have been lately snatched as brands from the burning; and ten have been added to the Society... The first meeting place was a cottage, now occupied by Mr J. Whiskerd where an attempt was made more than once to break up the meeting by the letting loose of sparrows – a favourite practice in those days, for which the culprits of East Bradenham had to answer in a court of Justice.

Mileham was the possessor of two chapels, the smaller of the two being the Wesleyan chapel situated in the Tittleshall Road, and dating from 1840. This building is in an excellent state of repair, due to the renovations brought about and interest shown in the building by the present owner, Mr Gold. The larger building was the meeting-place of Mileham Primitive Methodists. The foundation stone, dated 1886, is still visible and this chapel is situated in Back Lane.

A view of Back Street, Litcham, showing the Wesleyan chapel on the left.

Sunday School group. The picture includes: *Burton, Colman, Scott, Read, Moore, Easter, Wagg, Read, Colman, Moore, Gott, Moore, Manning, Clarke, Colman, Archer, Yeoman, Gott, Sater, Butcher, Bailey, Gott, Colman, Goddard, Walker, Walker, Askew.*

Mileham nativity play, c.1960. The photograph includes: *Mrs Betts, Percy Prior, Peter Hall, Edna Tuck, Pauline Bell, Revd Squires, Mrs Cheyney, Martin Godrick, Judy Ward, Jill Edge, Sheila Prior, Josephine Prior, Madelaine Prior, Jean Dye, Ann Moulton, Revd Walters, Dick Goderson, Donald Eason.*

SEVEN

THE VILLAGE SCHOOLS

SCHOOLS IN THE VILLAGE OF LITCHAM

1835–44
John Bridgeman (Parish Clerk) ran a school where Spurgeon's shop used to stand on the corner of Front Street and Church Street, now the green.

1836
Miss Ann Taylor ran a girls' boarding school, location and duration not known.

1845–90
Mrs Emma Warren ran a private school for young ladies in Front Street (known as the College), possibly in the present Bevan House.

1845–90
A private needlework school is believed to have operated at Chalk Farm in Druids Lane.

1845–1932
The Litcham village school (later the National School) taught students of all ages, in what is now the Jubilee Hall.

1900–11
Mrs Copeman ran a girls' boarding school at The Limes in Mileham Road.

1932
The primary school portion of the New Area School became operative, located between Church Street and Druids Lane.

1939
The Area School was completed and operational; this was later to become a secondary modern school.

1963
The county primary school opened adjacent to the Wellingham and Weasenham Roads Y-junction.

1963
With the opening of the county primary school the secondary modern school became a county high school.

Left: Honour award for good attendance, 1917–18, given to Abel Spencer.

Aerial view of Litcham School, 1932.

The school in Church Street, c.1930.

Litcham School, 1924. Left to right, back row: *Miss Read (teacher), D. Whittingdon, H. Boldero, J. Clarke, J. Hooks, ? Woodhouse;* middle: *C. Moore, C. Feeke, W. James, P. Warnes, K. Hooks, F. Winterbottom, L. Collison, E. Fulcher, W. Smith, R. Powley;* front: *J. Gibson, E. Gibson, E. Holland, E. Codling, P. Wakefield, G. Bensley, E. Fitheridge, S. Catton, J. Claxton, L. Codling.*

Litcham School, 1865. The headmaster was Mr Polkinhorne.

Litcham School, 1928. The schoolmaster was H. Frowen.

The school in 1929/30. Left to right, back: Ivy Pearson, S. Catton, Alice Hartley, D. Rye, D. Ward, J. Claxton, H. Yaxley; middle: P. Makins, Elsie Fuller, B. Codling, R. Breeze, D. Reeve, B. Potter, M. Spurgeon, E. Fitheridge; front: Adela Feeke, J. Moore, ? Bensley, P. Collison, E. Crane, K. Wagg.

Domestic science classes, 1933. Note the kerosene ovens.

School play, 1937. The photograph includes: K. Carter, D. Anthony, Rita Yallop, Joan Fitt,
Willie Melton, ? Lynn, B. Feeke, Maisie Carter, M. Smith, K. Ewen.

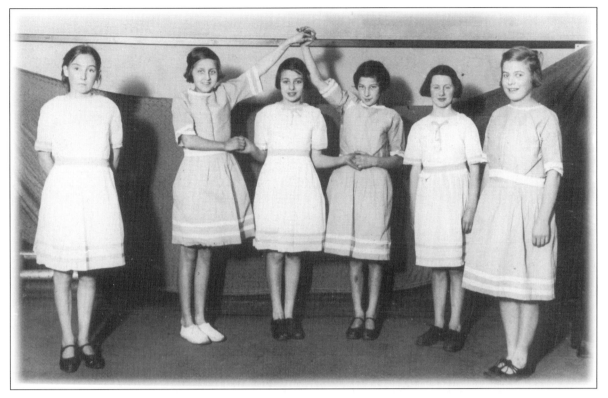

School play, 1937. Picture includes: P. Knock, O. Read, J. Codman, E. Twite, C. Feeke.

Litcham School, 1939. Left to right, boys: Derek Knock, Keith Carter, Norman Wagg, Leslie Bensley, Maurice Smith, Bertie Starr; girls: Doris Mickleborough, Silvia Anthony, Betty Linge, Peggy Mindham.

Above: *School teachers, 1950.* The masters are, left to right: *Messrs Petch, Heaton, Fronen, Reid, Symons;* and the mistresses: *Petch, Hubbard, Bates, Hall, Knock.*

Left: *Mr Addy, headmaster 1958–72.*

Right: *Litcham High School Band, 1977.*

Litcham Primary School, 1976. Craig Barnes, David Barnes, Joel ?, Robert Slegg, Justin Allen, Melanie Kerr, Victoria Sheraston, Julie Swain, Sadie Smith, Tracey Barnes, Denise Winterbone, Doreen Hurst, Marie Starling, Tina Savoury, Gail Hitchcock, Marion Howling, Tracey Fulcher, Michelle Smid, Kirsty Stoner, Gary Battleday, Leslie Raven, Christopher Blys, Mark Emery, Ross Kerr, Trevor Cross, Sam Stoner, Angela Madden, Tina Peeke, Georgina Cross, Susan Royal, Trevor Smith, Clarke Bullock, Nicola Hudson, Douglas Croll, Paul Masselis, Anthony Collin, Justin Bell, Paul Coleman, Jasmin Hargreaves, James Garner, Joanne Bowles, Catherine Martin, Lisa Warman, Dawn Dack, Gary Fulcher, Sharon Moore, Bret Evans, Darren Webster.

Litcham Secondary School senior football team, 1966–67 season. Left to right, back row: Richard Cross, Tommy Barnes, Malcolm Calaby, Graham Moore, Neville Hooks, Malcolm Whales, Mr R. Woodhouse; front: Clive Warnes, Neville Marsh, Bryan Hall, Jimmy Ogilvy, Robert Reeve.

Litcham Primary School, 1986. Left to right, back: *C. Purniss, M. Pickering, D. Mason, Mrs J. Woodhouse, A. Feeme, G. Chishome, S. Winterbone;* middle: *H. Dack, M. Gattuso, T. Payne, J. Pearson, T. Green, C. Thoday, L. Tyler;* front: *L. Gattuse, N. Forrest, M. Oldfield, K. Smedley, C.M. Tenell, L. Clements, L. Moore.*

Litcham Primary School, 1998. Left to right, back: *S. Mitchell, M. Norwell, C. Dennett, E. Dorman, J. Drake, C. Brown, Mrs J. Woodhouse;* middle: *S. Villaris, N. Binda, C. Goodrum, A. Skipper, N. Hayden, A. Walpole, H. Crane, S. Parmer,* front: *C. Reeve, T. Siggins, G. Glover, M. Cotterell, D. Thurgill, K. Jenkins, G. Wage, L. Barnes, J. Simpson.*

LITCHAM SCHOOL 150TH ANNIVERSARY

Litcham School celebrated the 150th anniversary of its opening on Sunday 15 and Monday 16 October 1995. A commemorative exhibition and reunion was organised with many former pupils attending the school, now the Jubilee Hall, on the Sunday. The exhibition included old writing slates and punishment books as well as a number of photographs, some of which dated from as early as the 1860s. The present village schools' pupils also took part, dressing in Victorian costume and being taught about past schooling methods.

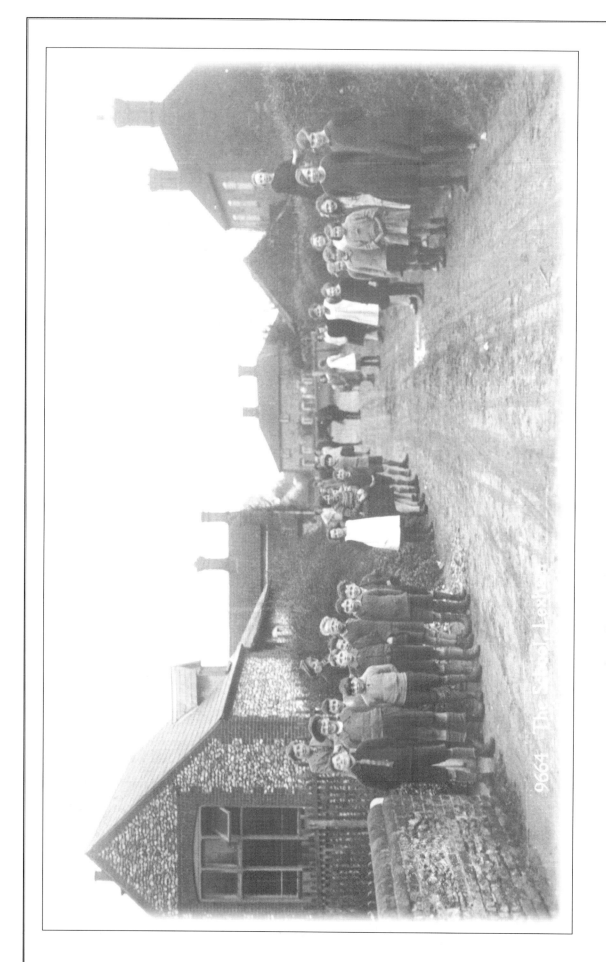

9664 - The School, Lexham

Street Farm Road, Lexham; the school has since been demolished.

LEXHAM SCHOOL

The school building that once stood in the village of East Lexham was pulled down some time around the middle of the twentieth century. There are no available records remaining from the school and no registers from which to draw information. Litcham School was built in 1932 and it is thought that it was around this time that the school in East Lexham began to run down. One of the teachers at East Lexham was Miss Pogson and there is a cottage named after her in the village today.

Lexham School seniors, 1930. Miss E. Radford is the headmistress.
The girls in Guide dress are the Crane family.

East Lexham School play.

The dancers at East Lexham School, c.1923–33.

School production of A Midsummer Night's Dream, *Lexham.*

MILEHAM SCHOOL

Mileham is perhaps best known as the birthplace of Sir Edward Coke who was born in the Old Hall in 1551. He was appointed Recorder of Norwich and later of London. After a successful political career as both Solicitor-General to Queen Elizabeth I and Lord Chief Justice under King James I, Sir Edward Coke died at the age of 83. It was during this period that a school in Mileham was first mentioned. Money was deposited with Sir Edward to purchase land and a house in which to begin a Free school founded by Allan Elwyn. There is little concrete information about the school before 1677 and Mileham School was established as an English School on 17 October of that year.

For a number of years prior to 1833, 17 children had been taught free at the school. In February a new system was adopted by which poor children of the parish were able to attend the school on payment of one penny per week. In 1875 a school board was established with the aim of providing a new school for the children. In 1876 the estimate for the cost of building the present school was £250 which rose to £465 by 1878. In the 1880s the number of pupils attending the school rose to 102 and in 1906 there were 120 children recorded. By 1937 the numbers had decreased dramatically to 53. The attendance fluctuated for a variety of reasons, and there were often bouts of illness at the school so many children were forced to stay at home. At certain points throughout the year children would be kept out of school to help with farming, harvesting and blackberry-picking. The arrival of evacuees during the war years also altered the numbers.

At the time of writing Mileham Primary School has 35 pupils, which is a vast improvement on the 23 children that attended in 2001. The headmistress at the school is Mrs Nightingale and there is one full-time teacher called Mrs Howard. There are also a number of valuable teaching assistants who together work to keep the school active. Mileham School has now provided the village with more than 300 years' of continuous education.

Mileham School, 1936. Group of boys, front to back, starting from right: *Frank Wilkin, Bob Walpole, Harry Wilkin, Tony Goderson, ?, John Russell, Lionel Stocks, Jessie Webster, Russell Rice, Bob Prior, Stanley Wilkin, Chris Williams, Harry Thurston, Frank Cason, Douglas Brown, Arthur Brown, Desmond Eagle, Isaac Burton, Tom Ward, Billy Newson, Gordon MacCullen;* infants, front: *David Walpole, Arthur Winterbone, Freddy Williams, Jean Custance, ?, Molly Poole, ?, ?, Molly Bell, Margaret Dady, Hilda Butcher, Joan Keens, Philip Prior, Brian Bell, Heather Kemp;* back: *Miss Mabel Bell (infant teacher), Gladys Dalton, Joan Burton, Edna Winterbone, Miss Gwen Forder (junior teacher), Brenda Cason, Hilda Rye, Eileen Webster, Doris Edge, Kathleen Webster, Eddie Webster, Eva Russell, Ruth Sewell, Joyce Walpole, Joyce Webster, Beryl Butcher, Mary Smith, Kathleen Vurley.*

Mileham School, 1933.

Mileham School. Left to right, back row: *Harry Elliott, Keith Downs, Joseph Peet, David Walpole, Geoffrey Cason, Wentworth Winterbone, Brian Goderson;* centre: *Dennis Gricks, Eddie Geegan, Chris Williams, Arthur Winterbone, Ronald Vurley, Freddie Williams;* front: *Kenny Stacey, Heather Kemp, Molly Bell, Pam Walpole, Mrs Forder, June Goderson, Kathy Elliot, Beryl Taylor, Barry Russell.*

Mileham School. Left to right, back row: *Raymond Nutman, Peter Brooks, Chris Williams, Clifford Wheeler, John Houghton, John Calaby;* centre: *Ronald Vurley, Jean Stearman, Heather Kemp, Mrs Fisher (head teacher), Beryl Taylor, Margaret Dady, Geoffrey Cason;* front: *David Walpole, Joseph Peet, Freddy Williams.*

HEAD TEACHERS AT MILEHAM SCHOOL, 1619–1977

Allan Elwyn	before 1619	F.S. Wigg	1906–08
Nicholas Yemes	1677	J. Licence	1908–15
Habakkuk Hensby	1760	A.C. Payne	1915–16
Joseph Kirby	1845	Mrs Payne	1916–19
H. Hammond	1875–86	Mrs Hilton (later E. Fisher)	1919–47
Mr Tidd	1886–1901	Mrs E. Cheyney	1947–66
W.M. Roberts	1901–03	Miss Osborn	1966–69
E.G. Everard	1903–06	A.D. Howard	1969–

Mileham School, 1941. Left to right, back row: *?, Peter Brooks, Clifford Wheeler, Chris Williams, John Calaby, Freddy Williams, Eddie Geegan;* centre: *Ronald Vurley, Billy Large, Rosina Clark, Heather Kemp, Beryl Taylor, Margaret Dady, David Walpole, Joseph Peet;* front: *Geoffrey Cason, Olive Starr, Molly Bell, Mrs Fisher (head teacher), Jean Custance, Edith Hawes, ?.*

Left: *Mileham School pupils in costume for the school play.*

Mileham School. Left to right, back row: *Albert Gould, Leslie Walpole, Julian Cason, Peter Bell, Tony Butcher, Johnathon Andrews, Jimmy Owen, William Haverson, Bobby Forbes, Graham Negus, Rodney Traites, Nigel Custance, Michael Russell;* third row: *Madelaine Prior, Pauline Bell, Josephine Prior, Evelyn Easter, Janice Easter, Barbara Owen, Pat Carter, Phylis Pearson;* second row: *Maureen Brown, Sandra Negus, Shirley Eastoe, Jill Edge, Judy Ward, Anita Butcher, Sandra Stacey, Sheila Prior, Angela Garner, Ann Moulton, Daphne Andrews;* front: *Brian Mortimer, Tony Owen, John Archer, Keith Easter, Terry Gray, Peter Shalomaki, Martin Goodrick, Michael Eagle, Christopher Taylor.* Teachers: *Miss Forder and Mrs Cheyney.*

EIGHT

SPORTS TEAMS & SOCIETIES

LITCHAM BRASS BAND

The idea of founding a band in Litcham was first discussed during a cricket match in the park at Lexham against Brisley in the summer of 1912. Mr Harold Player, who was then about to move from Brisley to Litcham as schoolmaster, was at the match and agreed to form a band when he took up his new appointment. The band began training in the winter of 1912/13 and did its marching in the meadow behind the schoolmaster's house (Hutlea, Church Street) where the original photograph *(reproduced below)* was taken in 1915. The band's first public engagement was at a garden fête in Scarning on that memorable day, 4 August 1914. Like so many organisations, the band was badly affected by the war with many of the members being called up. However, it was able to reform afterwards and continued for some years into the 1920s.

Litcham Brass Band, 1912. Left to right, back row: *James Knock, Robert Symonds, Arthur Howard, Billy Warnes, ? Hooks, Ernest Banham, Fred Banham, Fred Claxton, William Knock;* seated on chairs: *George Warnes, Harold Player, Jimmy Tilney;* seated on ground: *Charlie Howard, George Pratt.*

Revd Bartlett collecting ladies for tennis outside Litcham Rectory, 1906.

The Bull bowling green, 1926. Miss Porter, Miss Hubbard and Miss Singleton.

The 1951 darts team. Left to right, back: J. Webdale, K. Searle, C. Morrit, R. Moore, R. Cross, B. Williams, F. Feeke; front: I. Bennet, E. Fulcher, T. Howe, T. Fulcher.

Queen Mary and the Prince of Wales at the hunt.

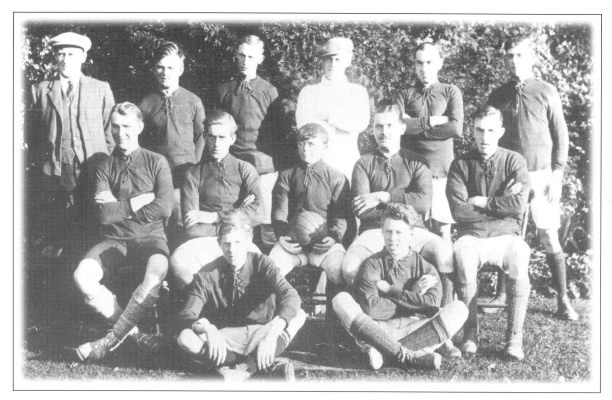

Litcham football club, The Wanderers, 1930. Left to right, back: Messrs Claxton, Mobbs, Martin, Pratt, Read, Yeoman; centre: Norton, Loades, Starr, Fisher, Symons; front: ?, Skipper: Day.

Below: *Football team, 1951/52. Left to right, back: Tony Howe, Ray Butcher, F. Feeke, B. Stearman, Neil Aulden; front: Barry Russell, ? Cheyney, Roy Stearman, Evan Fulcher, R. Cross and Colin Easter.*

Fancy dress mixed football team. Left to right, back: *Hilton, Dal, ?, Sandall, Smith, Colman;* middle: Mary *Harris, Askew. Among the remaining people in the picture are Breeze, Colman and Mobbs.*

Below: *Litcham cricket team, 1930.* The photograph includes: *Messrs King, Sandall, Swinger, King, Woodhouse, West, Ewing, Mobbs, Dixon, Woodhouse, Dixon.*

Lexham cricket team, 1970. Left to right, back: *Mr Wilkin, John Moore, T. Wilkin, Mr Howard,*
Mr Bambridge, Mr Merriweather, Gerald Fulcher, Mrs Wilkin; middle: *Fred Woodhouse, Mr McCormack,*
Mr Bailey, Mr Sayer, Mr Moore; front: *Mr Durrant, Mr Askew, Mr Moore, Mr Palmer, Mr Bambridge;*
on ground: *Skipper: Mr Bodimeade*

Lexham cricket team, 1984. Left to right, back: *Messrs Utting, Spencer, Palmer, Whitwood, Ogilvy, Askew;*
front: *Whitwood, Howell, Whitwood, Rallison, Green.*

Above: *Mileham cricket team, 1950.*

Below: *Lexham cricket team, 1948.* Pictured are: *Jimmy Everett* (far left, back), *F. Rackham* (next in line),
Billy Dixon (far right, back), *Freddy Oldfield* (middle row, hat), *H. Moore* (front, far left), *John Woodhouse*
(middle row, right), *Bob Creed* (front, far right).
Also included are: *S. Futter, B. Barney, R. Fiske, C. Harrowin.*

CLUBS & SOCIETIES

There are a number of clubs in the three villages as well as sports teams and social groups. There is the Litcham Historical & Amenity Society which is run by the Litcham Museum. There is a branch of the Royal British Legion and a Church Junior Leaders group. In Litcham the Youth Club is run by Mr R. Bailey and others. They have football teams aged up to 15 years and also cricket teams in the summer months, and the club holds a sports activity week each year during school holidays. Litcham also has a ladies group, a play group, a flower-arranging group and a dancing school which is run by Mrs D. Patterson. There is the opportunity for fishing in the nearby lakes and a number of other activities which keep the village alive and busy.

Right: *The Litcham Salvation Army, c.1907. John Codling and John Laws.*

Left: *Mileham Evergreen Club.*

Right: *Young farmers New Year dance in Dereham, 1970. Front left: Mr and Mrs Twite.*

WI presentation to Mrs Addy, c.1970.

Litcham Scouts, 1955. Left to right, back: R. Walpole, A. Pigstone, P. Mitchell, A. Webster, M. Coleman;
3rd row: J. Bodimeade, A. Colman, B. Lake, B. Beales, B. Clarke; 2nd row: M. Bishop, D. Williams, I. Gotts,
Mr Jepson, D. Lynn, R. Bullock; front: D. Martin, C. Archer, T. Moore.

Above: *Litcham Historical & Amenity Society Christmas party at Lexham Hall, 1998. Included are Mrs June Bevan, Mrs Kelly, Mrs D. Patterson, Mr and Mrs C. Archer, T. Riley, Mr and Mrs N.W.D. Foster (lord and lady of the manor), M. Colman, Mrs Shaw, Peter Hart, D. Moulton.*

Left: *The interior of Litcham Museum which houses the society's collection of photographs and artefacts.*

NINE
EVENTS & VILLAGE LIFE TODAY

LITCHAM TODAY

In 2002, Litcham is a thriving conservation village with both a high school and primary schools. It is served with a Post Office and general store, a corner shop, a butcher's and a fish-and-chip shop. The Jubilee Hall serves as the village hall and is used for many different functions by various clubs and groups within Litcham. The chapel and All Saints Church remain active parts of the community, as they have done for many years.

Many tradesmen still practise their crafts in Litcham, among them builders and architects. The village also boasts an up-to-date health centre. On market days there is a bus service to Fakenham, Swaffham and Dereham provided by Carter's Coaches. The company also serves Litcham for organised activities and outings.

Retirement party for Dr and Mrs Knappet, Litcham, 1975.

Group visit to Cadbury's, 1960.

Bus trip to the coast leaving from outside the sweet shop in Mileham (now North View).

Above: *Litcham firemen in Dereham Parade, 1939. B. Fitt is leading.*

Right: *The British Legion marching. PC Waters is in the foreground and Herbert Calaby is leading the procession, 1960.*

Above: *Advertisement for Litcham's celebrations of the 50th anniversary of VE Day, 1995.*

Top and right: *VE Day anniversary street party, Litcham, 1995.*

Litcham war memorial on the 50th anniversary of VE Day, 1995.

SUNDAY 20th AUGUST 1995

IN COMMEMORATION

of

V.J. DAY

&

THE END OF WORLD WAR II

AN ACT OF REMEMBRANCE CEREMONY

by

MEMBERS OF THE ROYAL BRITISH
LEGION

at

THE LITCHAM WAR MEMORIAL

at

2 pm

Followed by

An Exhibition

in the

LITCHAM VILLAGE MUSEUM

2 - 5 pm

Refreshments Available

Above: *Royal British Legion (Litcham Branch) President, Albert Calaby, to the left of standard-bearer Steven Lynn.*

Above: *Royal British Legion (Litcham Branch). The man in the background wearing the beret is Mr Jeremy, one of the oldest members of the Historical & Amenity Society.*

Left: *Advertisement for Litcham's VJ Day celebrations.*

Above: *Litcham Historical & Amenity Society member Peter Stoner in attendance on American jeep and wartime clothing at the VJ Day commemorative exhibition, 20 August 1995. The owner of the Jeep is Mr R.J. Mitchell. The event was held at Fourways, Litcham, the home of the Litcham Museum.*

Left: *Formation Badges of SEAC mounted and displayed by Litcham Historical & Amenity Society at VJ Day commemorative exhibition, 20 August 1995.*

Above: *Rector Jonathan Boston, N.W.D. Foster and Ron Shaw at the village fair, 1999.*

Right: *One of numerous stalls at Litcham village fair, 1999.*

Below: *Litcham village fair, 1999. Lord of the manor, N.W.D. Foster (left) is shown the floral displays in Litcham church by the rector, Jonathan Boston. Boston's father was Canon Boston of Dereham who wrote a history of Dereham.*

Children playing games at the village fête in Litcham in 2001.

Mrs Shaw and Vera Burchell enjoying Litcham village fête in 2001.

MILEHAM TODAY

Mileham is a pleasant Norfolk village situated along both sides of the B1145. It was mainly built around the old castle (a photograph of which can be seen on page 25). The population of the community has changed as little over hundreds of years as the impressive beauty of the buildings in the village.

Mileham has many amenities and services. These include a Post Office and general store and a nursery, a toddler group and a primary school for the village children. There is a village hall and the Church of St John the Baptist, which is situated at the north end of the village. There is also an active Women's Institute group and the Women's Fellowship as well as a Carpet Bowls Club. Two of the trades existing in the village in 2002 are Bells Transport and B. Beales Garage for vehicle resprays and repairs.

LEXHAM TODAY

At the time of writing, the picturesque Norfolk village of Lexham remains relatively unchanged. It is set in a peaceful valley with a river running through it and the centre of the settlement is marked by a butter market of recent make. There have been considerable renovations and improvements carried out in Lexham, many of these generated by the lord of the manor.

The village boasts an excellent children's play area and a beautiful Saxon round-tower church which is steeped in history. Lexham Hall opens its gardens twice a year for charity and it is a joy to stroll around and enjoy the layout of the grounds and the flowers in the magnificent garden. Despite having lost many services and trades over the years, Lexham is a thriving community.

Right: *Floats taking part in the Mileham celebrations for the Queen's Silver Jubilee, 1977.*

Left: *Mileham children playing at the bring-and-share picnic to celebrate the Queen's Golden Jubilee, 2002.*

SUBSCRIBERS

Mr F. Allan and Mrs June B. Bevan,
  Litcham, Norfolk
Miss Megan R. Angell, Litcham, Norfolk
Timothy and Helen Angell, Litcham,
  Norfolk
Miss Bethany R.H. Angell, Litcham,
  Norfolk
Mr and Mrs George Anthony, Litcham,
  Norfolk
Pamela M. Arnold, Kings Lynn, Norfolk
Winifred Askew, E. Lexham, Norfolk
Susan Laws Baccino, Aldeburgh, Suffolk
Sadie Bailey, Litcham, Norfolk
Richard G.J. Bailey
Mr and Mrs P.F. Ball, Litcham, Norfolk
Gemma J. Beales, Mileham, Norfolk
Nora Bell (née Oldfield), Necton, Norfolk
N.A. Bertram, Kempstone
Doreen Blyth, Great Massingham, Norfolk
The Reverend Jonathan Boston, Litcham,
  Norfolk
Ernest Boulton, West Lexham, Norfolk
H.F. and D.F. Bowman, Rougham
Gary Bridgewood, Litcham, Norfolk
Raymond Bullock, East Lexham, Kings
  Lynn, Norfolk
David S. Burton, Whissonsett, Norfolk
Sheila and Norman Burton, Litcham,
  Norfolk
Keith Trevor Carter
Christine Chalk, Litcham, Norfolk
Mr Stanley G. Chandler, Pinner, Middlesex
Hazel Clarke, East Lexham
Roy and Diane Clarke, East Lexham,
  Norfolk
Alison P. Claxton, Whissonsett, Norfolk
Llewellyn Compton DFC

Gill E. Copeman, Gt Massingham, Norfolk
Cecil Creed, Rougham, Norfolk
Russell L. Creed, Castle Acre, Norfolk
Jane Cummins (née Knock), Bury St
  Edmunds, Suffolk
David and Cindy Dew, The Bungalow,
  Litcham, Norfolk
Maurice Dye, Dereham, Norfolk
Mr Stanley Eastoe, Sunnyside Farm,
  Mileham, Norfolk
Lynette Emerson, Mileham, Norfolk
Susan Emery, Litcham, Norfolk
Fredrick H. Feeke, Litcham, Norfolk
Peter C.P. Finney, Mileham, Norfolk
Josephine Fisher (nee Prior), formerly of
  Mileham
Mr F. Fitt, Litcham, Norfolk
Richard F. Foster, Manor House, Colkirk,
  Norfolk
Charles Foster, Cokesford Farm, Tittleshall,
  Norfolk
Neil W.D. Foster, Lexham Hall, Norfolk
Andrew C. Fulcher, Litcham, Norfolk
Nicholas I. Fulcher, Isle of Man
Joyce E. Fulcher, Litcham, Norfolk
Jeremy A. Fulcher, Sporle, Norfolk
Robert D. Fulcher
Mr and Mrs Jack Goderson, Mileham,
  Norfolk
Kathy and Tony Gray, Mileham, Norfolk
Trevor Green, East Lexham, Norfolk
D.R. Gricks, Mileham, Norfolk
Pamela S. Griffin, West Lexham, Norfolk
Jean M. Grimmer (née Constable),
  Hertfordshire
Eileen M. Grimmer (née Constable),
  Dersingham, Norfolk

Gary Haigh Smith and Clara du Cann, Jesters Barn, Mileham, Norfolk

Mr and Mrs M. Hamer, Garden House, Lexham Hall, Norfolk

John Hamilton, Mileham, Norfolk

Judith M. Harrison (née Hooks), Litcham, Norfolk

Chris, Elaine and Eleanor Hebden, Bramley Cottage, Great Dunham

Cdr Huib van Hoeven

John F. Hooks, Litcham, Norfolk

Mrs James Simpson, Miss A., Miss J, and Miss I. Hovenden-Simpson,

Mrs Rosemary A. Howard, Mileham, Norfolk

Ted Howe, Litcham, Norfolk

David Hunter, Mileham, Norfolk

Rachel Jane Jones, born Litcham Priory 1968

Sarah Jean Jones, born Litcham Priory 1966

Benjamin Jenkin Jones, born Litcham Priory 1972

Deborah Joyce Helen Jones, born Litcham Priory 1965

Mrs Dorothy M. Joyce, Litcham/Mileham

Morris and Christine Julian, Mileham, Norfolk

Sharon Junge (née Smith), Dereham, Norfolk

Miss J. and D. Knock, Toftwood, Dereham

Mr John H. Laffey, Litcham, Norfolk

Victoria Lawrence, Litcham, Norfolk

Edwin John and Celia Laws, Litcham, Norfolk

Rene Le-Roux (née Oldfield), Canada

Litcham CP School

Mark and Sue Lowther, Litcham, Norfolk

Derrick George Lynn, Litcham, Norfolk

John J. Madden, Litcham, Norfolk

George and Karen Martinez, Abilene, Texas

Mrs Rose Melton, Peterborough

David A.R. Milligan, born Litcham/Swanton Morley, Norfolk

T.J. Moore, Sculthorpe, Litcham, Norfolk

John and Elaine Moore, Necton, Norfolk

Margaret Moore (née Warnes), Litcham, Norfolk

Bob Morgan, Mileham, Norfolk

Ronnie and Nancy Myhill, Elsing, Norfolk

Bob Nash, Great Massingham, Norfolk

Elsie M. Ogilvy, Litcham, Norfolk

Michael and Lynda Oldfield, Litcham, Norfolk

Margaret Oldfield (née Feeke), Litcham, Norfolk

Christopher Paice, Odd Fellows Hall, Litcham, Norfolk

Jake Mark Parker, Beeston, Norfolk

Helen Paterson, Castle Acre, Norfolk

Lt Col (Ret'd) and Mrs M.D. Patterson, Litcham, Norfolk

Susan Payne, Litcham, Norfolk

Amy Pearson, Hilgay, Norfolk

Pam Pearson (née Walpole), Mileham, Norfolk

Des and Janice Pickering, East Lexham, Norfolk

Joyce P. Prior, Mileham, Norfolk

John M. Rayner, Ely, Cambridgeshire

Peter and Janice Riches, Westfield, Dereham, Norfolk

Angela Rix (née Savory)

Nigel and Robin Roberson, Tittleshall, Norfolk

Mr K.T. Rye, Weasenham, Norfolk

Leonard G. Sayer, Litcham, Norfolk

Ken Smalley, Rougham

Mrs J.E. Smith, Litcham, Norfolk

Stephen and Diane Spencer (née Fitt), Great Dunham, Norfolk

Mr and Mrs S. Taylor, Litcham, Norfolk

Ernest E. Thompson (Burton family)

Gerald M. Thompson (Burton family), Hellesdon, Norfolk

Barry Tomlin, Mileham, Norfolk

Mike Tomlin, Mileham, Norfolk

Mary K. Tompkins, Litcham, Norfolk

Maurice J. Tooke, Rainham, Essex

Mike and Phyllis Troupe, Litcham Post Office

Charles W. Utting

Liz and Godfrey Valentine, Mileham, Norfolk

Christine J. Wall, Mileham, Norfolk

John F.W. Walling, Newton Abbot, Devon

Mr G.A. Walpole, Whissonsett, Norfolk

Albert Walpole, Mileham, Norfolk

Mr and Mrs P. Warnes, Litcham, Norfolk

'Blue' Will Webster, Mileham, Norfolk

Mrs Edna Whales, Great Dunham, Norfolk

Master Thomas White, Litcham, Norfolk

Mr and Mrs G. Whitwood, Litcham, Norfolk

Mrs Edna F. Winterbone

Chris and Lindsey Wood, Litcham, Norfolk

Titles from the Series

The Book of Addiscombe • Various
The Book of Addiscombe, Vol. II • Various
The Book of Bampton • Caroline Seward
The Book of Barnstaple • Avril Stone
Book of Bickington • Stuart Hands
Blandford Forum: A Millennium Portrait • Various
The Book of Bridestowe • R. Cann
The Book of Brixham • Frank Pearce
The Book of Buckland Monachorum & Yelverton • Hemery
The Book of Carshalton • Stella Wilks
The Parish Book of Cerne Abbas • Vale & Vale
The Book of Chagford • Ian Rice
The Book of Chittlehamholt with
Warkleigh & Satterleigh • Richard Lethbridge
The Book of Chittlehampton • Various
The Book of Colney Heath • Bryan Lilley
The Book of Constantine • Moore & Trethowan
The Book of Cornwood & Lutton • Various
The Book of Creech St Michael • June Small
The Book of Cullompton • Various
The Book of Dawlish • Frank Pearce
The Book of Dulverton, Brushford,
Bury & Exebridge • Various
The Book of Dunster • Hilary Binding
The Ellacombe Book • Sydney R. Langmead
The Book of Exmouth • W.H. Pascoe
The Book of Grampound with Creed • Bane & Oliver
The Book of Hayling Island & Langstone • Rogers
The Book of Helston • Jenkin with Carter
The Book of Hemyock • Clist & Dracott
The Book of Hethersett • Various
The Book of High Bickington • Avril Stone
The Book of Ilsington • Dick Wills
The Book of Lamerton • Ann Cole & Friends
Lanner, A Cornish Mining Parish • Scharron Schwartz &
Roger Parker
The Book of Leigh & Bransford • Various
The Book of Litcham with Lexham & Mileham • Various
The Book of Loddiswell • Various
The Book of Lulworth • Rodney Legg

The Book of Lustleigh • Joe Crowdy
The Book of Manaton • Various
The Book of Markyate • Richard Hogg
The Book of Mawnan • Various
The Book of Meavy • Pauline Hemery
The Book of Minehead with Alcombe • Binding & Stevens
The Book of Morchard Bishop • Jeff Kingaby
The Book of Newdigate • John Callcut
The Book of Northlew with Ashbury • Various
The Book of North Newton • Robins & Robins
The Book of North Tawton • Various
The Book of Okehampton • Radford & Radford
The Book of Paignton • Frank Pearce
The Book of Penge, Anerley & Crystal Palace • Various
The Book of Peter Tavy with Cudlipptown • Various
The Book of Pimperne • Jean Coull
The Book of Plymtree • Tony Eames
The Book of Porlock • Denis Corner
Postbridge – The Heart of Dartmoor • Reg Bellamy
The Book of Priddy • Various
The Book of Rattery • Various
The Book of Silverton • Various
The Book of South Molton • Various
The Book of South Stoke • Various
South Tawton & South Zeal with Sticklepath • Radfords
The Book of Sparkwell
with Hemerdon & Lee Mill • Pam James
The Book of Staverton • Pete Lavis
The Book of Stithians • Various
The Book of Studland • Rodney Legg
The Book of Swanage • Rodney Legg
The Book of Torbay • Frank Pearce
Uncle Tom Cobley & All: Widecombe-in-the-Moor • Stephen
Woods
The Book of Watchet • Compiled by David Banks
The Book of West Huntspill • Various
Widecombe-in-the-Moor • Stephen Woods
The Book of Williton • Michael Williams
Woodbury: The Twentieth Century Revisited • Roger Stokes
The Book of Woolmer Green • Various

Forthcoming

For details of any of the above titles or if you are
interested in writing your own history, please contact: Commissioning Editor Community Histories,
Halsgrove House, Lower Moor Way, Tiverton Business Park, Tiverton, Devon EX16 6SS, England;
email: naomic@halsgrove.com

In order to include as many historic photographs as possible in this volume, a printed index is not included. However, the Community History Series is indexed by Genuki. For further information and indexes to volumes in the series, please visit:
http://www.cs.ncl.uk/genuki/DEV/indexingproject.html